COUNTRIES OF THE WORLD

South Africa

Gareth Stevens Publishing
A WORLD ALMANAC EDUCATION GROUP COMPANY

About the Author: Mary-Ann Stotko obtained her honor's degree in English from the University of South Africa. She has taught English in South Africa, Germany, and Singapore and is currently working on her master's degree.

PICTURE CREDITS
Allsport/Mike Powell: 37 (bottom)
A.N.A. Press Agency: 5, 9 (top), 36, 66, 71 (top), 83
Andes Press Agency: 14 (bottom), 23, 24, 70, 77
Archive Photos: 84
Bes Stock: cover, 6, 32, 35, 71 (bottom), 87, 89
Camera Press: 4, 8, 61
The Canadian Press Picture Archive: 76, 79, 82
Alain Evrard: 20, 30, 43, 69, 72, 91
Getty Images/HultonArchive: 12, 14 (top), 15 (top), 15 (bottom), 57 (top), 75, 78, 80
Hans Hayden: 2, 7 (bottom), 9 (bottom), 42, 46 (top), 52, 73
The Hutchison Library: 19, 22, 25, 40, 41 (bottom)
iAfrika: 13, 15 (center), 28, 54, 64
Images of Africa Photobank: 3 (bottom), 44 (both), 45, 56, 57 (bottom), 58 (both)
Imapress: 29 (left)
Earl Kowall: 68, 74
Jason Lauré: 18, 38, 39 (top), 59, 65
Liaison Agency: 17
North Wind Picture Archives: 10, 11, 47, 63
Christine Osborne Pictures: 26, 33 (top)
Mary-Ann Stotko: 90
Topham Picturepoint: 3 (top), 3 (center), 7 (top), 29 (right), 34, 39 (bottom), 46 (bottom), 48, 50, 55, 60, 62, 81, 85
Trip Photographic Library: 1, 16, 21, 27, 31, 33 (bottom), 37 (top), 41 (top), 49, 51, 53, 67

Digital Scanning by Superskill Graphics Pte Ltd

Written by
MARY-ANN STOTKO

Edited by
KATHARINE BROWN

Edited in the U.S. by
PATRICIA LANTIER
MONICA RAUSCH

Designed by
ROSIE FRANCIS

Picture research by
SUSAN JANE MANUEL

First published in North America in 2002 by
Gareth Stevens Publishing
A World Almanac Education Group Company
330 West Olive Street, Suite 100
Milwaukee, Wisconsin 53212 USA

Please visit our web site at
www.garethstevens.com
For a free color catalog describing
Gareth Stevens' list of high-quality books
and multimedia programs, call
1-800-542-2595 (USA) or
1-800-461-9120 (CANADA).
Gareth Stevens Publishing's
Fax: (414) 332-3567.

© **TIMES MEDIA PRIVATE LIMITED 2002**
Originated and designed by
Times Editions
An imprint of Times Media Private Limited
A member of the Times Publishing Group
Times Centre, 1 New Industrial Road
Singapore 536196
http://www.timesone.com.sg/te

Library of Congress Cataloging-in-Publication Data
Stotko, Mary-Ann.
South Africa / by Mary-Ann Stotko.
p. cm. — (Countries of the world)
Includes bibliographical references and index.
Summary: Provides an overview of the geography, history, government, language, art, and food of South Africa, exploring its customs and current issues.
ISBN 0-8368-2347-8 (lib. bdg.)
1. South Africa—Juvenile literature. [1. South Africa.] I. Title.
II. Countries of the world (Milwaukee, Wis.)
DT1719.S76   2002
968–dc21   2001049070

Printed in Malaysia

1 2 3 4 5 6 7 8 9 06 05 04 03 02

Contents

AN OVERVIEW OF SOUTH AFRICA

The Republic of South Africa, the "Rainbow Nation," is a large, beautiful, resource-rich land with a turbulent history that dates back to humankind's beginnings. Situated at the southernmost tip of the African continent, South Africa is a country of contrasts, with varied climatic zones, many kinds of flora and fauna, an abundance of minerals, and a variety of cultures.

Today, South Africa is emerging from a time of turmoil that began when European explorers first discovered the country's economic potential. Long shunned for its political system of racial segregation known as *apartheid* (ah-PAHRT-hate), South Africa reentered the world community in the 1990s, this time as a democratic nation.

Opposite: **Cape Town's architecture is a mixture of traditional buildings and modern skyscrapers. The buildings near the city's Victoria and Albert Waterfront are set against a backdrop of rugged mountains.**

Below: **These young South Africans in Cape Town have a bright future in multiethnic South Africa.**

THE FLAG OF SOUTH AFRICA

The current flag of South Africa was first flown on April 27, 1994. The flag has a blue-black triangle that is vertical to the flagpole and bordered in gold. Bands of green, white, red, and blue appear horizontally. The flag's colors are the principal colors that have been used in the country's various flags since 1652. The two green stripes that flow into one symbolize the reconciliation and the convergence of South Africa's past and its future. The flag's theme of convergence and unity ties in with the motto on the national coat of arms, "Unity in Diversity."

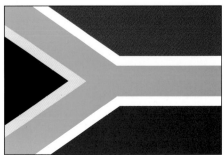

Geography

Located at the southernmost tip of the continent of Africa, South Africa covers an area of 471,008 square miles (1,219,912 square kilometers). The country is bordered by Namibia to the northwest, Botswana and Zimbabwe to the north, Mozambique to the northeast, and Swaziland to the east. The southeastern region surrounds the independent state of Lesotho. The Indian Ocean runs along South Africa's southern and eastern coasts, while the Atlantic Ocean is on the country's southwestern coast.

The Land

The South African landscape includes mountains, deserts, subtropical regions, savannas, and beaches. A mountainous ridge, known as the Great Escarpment, divides the country's coastal regions and interior plateau.

A narrow strip of land stretches for 1,739 miles (2,798 km) along the coast, while most of the country's interior is a saucer-like plateau. This plateau covers about two-thirds of South Africa and consists of three main areas of *veld* (FELT), or grassy plains: the Highveld, the Middleveld, and the Lowveld.

Ranging in elevation from about 4,000 to 6,000 feet (1,219 to 1,829 meters), the Highveld is the largest of the three veld areas. It is characterized by level or gently sloping terrain

Below: **The fertile plains of KwaZulu Natal stretch southwestward to the Drakensberg Mountains.**

that is covered with pans, or salt lakes. Land use in the Highveld varies from cattle grazing in the west to mixed farming (both crops and livestock) in the center to growing grain, especially corn, in the east. The northern boundary of this area is marked by a rock ridge called the Witwatersrand. Bounding the Highveld in the southeast, the Drakensberg Mountains, which form part of the Great Escarpment, contain the country's highest peak, Mount Njesuthi, at 11,182 feet (3,408 m).

Lying at an altitude of between 2,000 and 4,000 feet (610 and 1,219 m), the Middleveld is located west of the Highveld. The northernmost part of the Middleveld forms part of the Kalahari, a large, sand-covered, basinlike plain that stretches north into neighboring Namibia and Botswana. The Middleveld also contains the southernmost portion of the Kalahari Desert. The Lowveld covers the northeastern province of Mpumalanga and the northern part of KwaZulu Natal.

Rivers

The Orange River is South Africa's longest river. With a length of 1,300 miles (2,092 km), the river flows westward from its source in Lesotho before emptying into the Atlantic Ocean. Other major rivers are the Vaal and Limpopo rivers. Although the country has many rivers, none of them are navigable.

THE MYSTERY OF THE CAPE OF GOOD HOPE

Renowned for its ferocious weather and rough seas, the Cape of Good Hope (*below*) has wrecked many ships over the centuries and has also given rise to stories of phantom ships.
(A Closer Look, page 52)

Climate

Although most of South Africa enjoys a warm, temperate climate, the country experiences regional climatic variations. In the Atlantic Ocean, the cold, northward-flowing Benguela Current cools the western coast and contributes to the dryness of the western regions. The warm, southward-flowing Agulhas Current in the Indian Ocean keeps temperatures high on the eastern and southeastern coasts.

South Africa lies in the Southern Hemisphere, so the seasons occur at exactly opposite times of the year from those in North America and Europe. Summer lasts from December to February and winter from June through August. In summer, the weather is warm to hot, with daytime temperatures averaging between 70° to 90° Fahrenheit (21° to 32° Celsius). In winter, daytime temperatures average between 50° and 70° F (10° and 21° C). Temperatures at night, however, can fall below freezing in many of the country's high-altitude areas.

Annual rainfall in South Africa varies from less than 8 inches (20 centimeters) in the dry, northwestern region to more than 40 inches (102 cm) along the KwaZulu Natal coast.

Above: **Because most of South Africa enjoys a mild, sunny climate, wildflowers, such as these in Western Cape, bloom throughout the country.**

CONSERVATION

Conservation has been a serious issue in South Africa for decades and presents a dilemma in a country where the need for farmland conflicts with the desire to preserve nature.

(A Closer Look, page 44)

Plants and Animals

Vegetation in South Africa varies according to region. The dry areas in the western and central parts of the country contain hardy, succulent plants. Grasslands cover most of the interior plateau, while the northeastern region is made up of savanna vegetation, consisting of mixed grassland and bushes and trees, such as baobab and mopani trees. Only a small portion of natural forest remains and is situated in Mpumalanga and on the southern coast. KwaZulu Natal contains lush, dense subtropical evergreen trees and plants. Western Cape has a distinct vegetation of grasses, shrubs, and trees and is home to many of the country's twenty thousand species of flowering plants.

South Africa has a spectacular wildlife heritage. Many large animals, such as lions, elephants, zebras, leopards, monkeys, and rhinoceroses, are indigenous to the country. Smaller mammals include mongooses, jackals, and various cats. Bird life is abundant and includes ostriches and grouse. South Africa is also home to numerous reptile species, including over one hundred species of snakes, about one-fourth of which are poisonous.

THREE NATIONAL PARKS

About 5.5 percent of South Africa's land has been set aside to preserve the country's rich and varied plants and wildlife. The nation's largest park is Kruger National Park, which accommodates a large variety of animals, including the "Big Five" — rhinoceroses (*above*), lions, leopards, buffalo, and elephants.
(*A Closer Look*, page 66)

THE SOUTHERN RIGHT WHALE

Until the 1990s, the southern right whale was under the threat of extinction due to widespread hunting by humans.
(*A Closer Look*, page 64)

Left: The king protea, South Africa's national flower, is an unusual flower found nowhere else on Earth.

History

The land now known as South Africa was originally populated by San hunter-gatherers. These peoples were then joined by the Khoikhoi. Iron Age Bantu-speaking peoples migrated southward from central Africa and had settled in the Transvaal (now in northern South Africa) by A.D. 100. The Nguni, ancestors of the Zulu and Xhosa, occupied most of the eastern coast by 1500.

The Arrival of Europeans

The Portuguese were the first Europeans to round the Cape of Good Hope in 1488. The first settlement, however, was not established until 1652 by Dutchman Jan van Riebeeck. French and German Protestants joined the Dutch settlers in subsequent decades, and they became known collectively as the *Boers* (BOO-ers). Some whites married members of other groups, including the San; Khoikhoi; and Malays, who were brought to South Africa to work as slaves in the 1700s. The descendants of these unions formed a separate group of people, known as coloreds.

In 1795, British forces captured the settlement, known as the Cape Colony. They lost control of it in 1802 but recaptured it in 1806. Britain was granted the colony in the Treaty of Vienna in

EARLY CLASHES

During the second half of the seventeenth century, the Boer settlers in South Africa began cattle farming, which, in turn, led to the need for more grazing land. Consequently, the Boer settlements extended all over the southern part of the Cape (now located in Western Cape) and east toward the Fish River. In the area of the Fish River, the settlers encountered the populous, agricultural Xhosa people. By the end of the 1700s, minor cattle raids developed into frontier wars between the Boers and Xhosa. For nearly one hundred years, the Xhosa fought the Cape Colony settlers, first the Boers and later the British. Fighting continued until all Xhosa territories were incorporated into the Cape Colony.

Left: Seventeenth-century Dutch ships from Rotterdam set sail for the shores of South Africa's cape region (now located in Western Cape). The Dutch established their first settlement there as a stopping point for Dutch East India Company trading vessels on their way to the East.

Left: This is an artist's impression of an 1850s Boer farm in Orange Free State.

1814. British colonists began arriving in 1820. British settlement and rule marked the beginning of a long conflict between the Boers and the British. English became the official language of the colony, and slavery was abolished. These measures were bitterly resented by the Boers and led to the Great Trek, in which thousands of Boers migrated into the South African interior. Some Boers settled in Natal (now KwaZulu Natal), while others went north across the Vaal and Orange rivers. This migration brought the Boers into contact and conflict with African groups in the area.

In 1852 and 1854, the independent Boer republics of the Transvaal and Orange Free State (present-day Free State) were created. The discovery of diamonds in Orange Free State and gold in the Transvaal caused the republics' economies to boom and led to a mass influx of Europeans (mainly British) to these areas. Many Africans also moved into these areas to work in the mines. Mine owners constructed hostels for African workers that were completely separate from those of white workers and set patterns that later extended throughout the region.

From War to Union

The rise in British immigration and tension over unequal political rights for British immigrants led to the South African War in 1899. The British defeated the Boers in 1902, and the two Boer republics became part of the British Empire. In May 1910, the former Boer republics and the British colonies of the Cape and Natal formed the Union of South Africa, a self-governing country within the British Empire.

SHAKA, PRIDE OF THE WARRIOR ZULUS

In the early nineteenth century, a young prince named Shaka became chieftain of the Zulu tribe. Using unique warrior tactics, Shaka went on to create one of the mightiest empires the African continent has ever known.

(*A Closer Look*, page 60)

THE SOUTH AFRICAN WAR

Lasting two and a half years, the South African War, also known as the Boer War, was an expensive and brutal colonial war fought between Britain and the allied Boer republics of Transvaal and Orange Free State.

(*A Closer Look*, page 62)

On the Road to Apartheid

The union's constitution ensured all political power was in the hands of the white community. Under the leadership of Louis Botha and the South African Party (SAP), the government began introducing laws, called apartheid, that separated white and nonwhite South Africans in all aspects of life. As a reaction to these policies, black African leaders founded the South African Native National Congress, which later became known as the African National Congress (ANC).

During World War I, South Africa sided with Britain, and by 1915 South African soldiers had defeated German troops occupying South West Africa (modern Namibia). The League of Nations granted the former German colony to South Africa in 1919.

The Years of Apartheid

In 1948, the National Party (NP) came into power and continued the policy of apartheid. Designed to separate white and nonwhite South Africans in all arenas, apartheid led to white domination in a predominantly black society. Through successive governments, the NP extended and legalized white economic exploitation, political domination, and social privilege.

Left: White South African children wade in a pond in Pretoria National Botanical Gardens in the 1950s. During the years of apartheid, racial discrimination ruled everyday life. Signs, such as the one here, denoting which ethnic group could use particular facilities were displayed everywhere, including park benches, buses, beaches, restaurants, public restrooms, and libraries.

Left: In August 1989, lawyers, including Johnny de Lange (*second from left*) and Dulla Omar (*third from left*), took part in the Cape Town Defiance Campaign Against Apartheid. Protests such as this one became increasingly frequent as more and more South Africans demanded change.

By the 1950s, black South Africans began to actively oppose the government. Membership of the ANC grew under the leadership of Albert Luthuli and Nelson Mandela, and the Pan-Africanist Congress (PAC) was formed. Both groups were banned in 1960, following the police massacre of sixty-seven people in the black township of Sharpeville. The next year, South Africa left the Commonwealth, which opposed the country's severe racial policies, and declared itself a republic. The government maintained a hard line against its opponents, and by 1964 all political opposition leaders, including Nelson Mandela, had been imprisoned or killed or had fled the country.

Resistance to apartheid resurged in the 1970s, with the emergence of new protest groups and leaders, most notably Stephen Biko. In June 1976, thousands of black children in Soweto demonstrated against the compulsory use of the Afrikaans language in schools. Police opened fire, killing at least 174 students. Subsequent demonstrations were crushed brutally. Protests were renewed the following year after the death of Biko while he was in police custody. As a direct result of these events, the United Nations (U.N.) Security Council approved a compulsory arms embargo against South Africa.

THE INJUSTICES OF APARTHEID

Racial laws covered every aspect of South African life. The Group Areas Act of 1950 divided the country's cities and towns into segregated residential and business areas. Millions of black South Africans were forcibly removed from their homes and placed in one of ten homelands that each housed a specific African ethnic community. Indians and coloreds were forced to live in designated areas, too. Black South Africans were not permitted to spend more than seventy-two hours in white areas unless they worked there. They also had to carry passes ready for police inspection at all times. Interracial marriages were illegal.

The Weakening of Apartheid

By the end of the 1970s, the country's economy was in recession, skilled white South Africans were emigrating, and inflation was high. International criticism of the government's apartheid policy was also growing. As a result, the government of Prime Minister Pieter W. Botha adopted a new constitution that gave segregated representation to Indians and coloreds and gave great powers to the country's president. These measures, however, failed to meet black aspirations, and violence mounted as the black population demanded further change. By the mid-1980s, many Western countries had imposed economic sanctions against South Africa.

The Transition to a Democracy

In 1989, President F. W. de Klerk launched a series of reforms that speedily led to the release of ANC leader Nelson Mandela and other political prisoners. The ban on opposition groups and parties was also lifted, and a dialogue began between the government and these parties to bring about democracy in South Africa. In the same year, Namibia was granted its independence. The remaining apartheid laws were gradually dismantled, and the country's first democratic elections were held in 1994. The ANC became the majority party in a new parliament, and Nelson Mandela was sworn in as the country's president.

NELSON MANDELA

Nelson Mandela's twenty-seven-year imprisonment for his part in the ANC's antigovernment activities made him an international symbol for the struggle for freedom, as well as the world's most famous political prisoner. Sacrificing his personal freedom for nearly three decades, Mandela (*above*) became the first black president of a democratic South Africa in 1994.
(*A Closer Look, page 50*)

Left: **This South African shields his face from the sun as he watches the inauguration ceremony of Nelson Mandela as the country's first democratically elected president on May 10, 1994, in Pretoria.**

Christiaan Neethling Barnard (1922–2001)

Christiaan Neethling Barnard studied medicine and became a resident surgeon at Groote Schuur Hospital in Cape Town in 1953. After completing doctoral studies at the University of Minnesota, Barnard returned to work at the hospital. He introduced open-heart surgery to South Africa and developed a new design for artificial heart valves. He is most famous for being the first surgeon to perform a human heart transplant in 1967. Barnard retired from surgical practice in 1983 and was honored with the first world health award in November 2000.

Christiaan Neethling Barnard

Zensi Miriam Makeba (1932–)

Known as "Mama Africa," Zensi Miriam Makeba is one of the world's most prominent black African performers. Born in a segregated black township outside of Johannesburg in 1932, Makeba became a professional singer in 1954. By the late 1950s, her music was well known in South Africa. Due to her outspoken criticism of apartheid, Makeba's music was banned in South Africa, and she was forced into exile in 1960. Consequently, Makeba moved to the United States, where she embarked on a successful singing and recording career. Throughout her career, Makeba has also actively promoted humanitarian ideals, such as racial equality. Makeba returned to South Africa in 1990, after thirty years in exile.

Zensi Miriam Makeba

Desmond Mpilo Tutu (1931–)

Born in 1931, Desmond Mpilo Tutu became the first black South African to serve as dean of St. Mary's Cathedral in Johannesburg from 1975 to 1976. His outspoken criticism of racial discrimination and his constant appeal for equal rights for black South Africans made him a prominent public figure. He advocated nonviolent protest and promoted international sanctions against South Africa. For his role in the opposition to apartheid, Tutu was awarded the Nobel Prize for Peace in 1984. He became archbishop of Cape Town and head of the Anglican Church in South Africa in 1986. Archbishop Tutu retired from these positions in 1996 so he could devote himself to his role as head of the Truth and Reconciliation Commission, to which he had been appointed in 1995.

Desmond Mpilo Tutu

Government and the Economy

The South African Parliament adopted a temporary constitution in 1993, which was replaced by a permanent constitution in 1996. The 1996 constitution, which allows all South Africans to vote for members of Parliament (MPs), took effect over three years.

Today, South Africa is a republic whose government consists of legislative, executive, and judicial branches. The bicameral Parliament, or two-part legislative body, consists of the National Assembly and the National Council of Provinces. The National Assembly is made up of between 350 and 400 MPs, who serve five-year terms. The number of seats allocated to each party in the National Assembly is determined by the percentage of votes each party receives. The National Council of Provinces consists of ninety members. Ten members are elected by each of the country's nine provincial legislatures for five-year terms. The National Council of Provinces represents provincial interests at the national level.

The president is chosen from and elected by the National Assembly. Serving a five-year term, the president is the country's

THE TRUTH AND RECONCILIATION COMMISSION

The Truth and Reconciliation Commission (TRC) has helped advance the reconciliation process in South Africa. Chaired by Archbishop Desmond Tutu since it was established in 1995, the purpose of the commission has been threefold. TRC has investigated human rights abuses committed between 1960 and May 1994, granted amnesty to those who committed politically motivated crimes, and advised on compensation for victims of abuses.

Left: South Africa's Houses of Parliament are located in Cape Town, the legislative capital of the country. Built in Victorian architectural style, the main parliament building was completed in 1885. When the Union of South Africa was formed in 1910, the building became the seat of the country's national parliament.

Left: Thabo Mbeki, South Africa's current president, addresses Parliament at its first sitting of the year on February 4, 2000, in Cape Town.

chief of state and head of government. A cabinet assists the president in running the government. The president chooses the members of the cabinet and determines their duties. Consisting of a deputy president and the heads of government departments, the cabinet members are chosen mainly from the members of the National Assembly.

Provincial Government

Before 1994, South Africa was divided into four provinces and ten other areas, known as homelands. All of these were dissolved by the 1993 constitution and replaced with the current nine provinces. Each province has a premier. The premier presides over an executive council, which is made up of between five and ten members. These provincial councils can pass bills on many of the same matters as the national parliament, but their powers are more limited.

THE JUDICIARY SYSTEM

South Africa's judiciary system is independent from the legislative and executive branches. Consisting of a president and ten judges, the Constitutional Court is the country's highest court. The Supreme Court of Appeals is the country's highest court of appeal except in constitutional matters. South Africa also has a number of high courts. The country's lower courts are local courts run by magistrates and traditional leaders.

Economy

South Africa's economy suffered for years due to economic sanctions imposed by foreign countries in protest against the nation's system of apartheid. Since the end of apartheid in the early 1990s, however, the South African government has aimed to sustain economic growth and achieve a measure of industrial self-sufficiency. Today, the country has a mixed economy, with an agricultural sector, great mineral wealth, and a diverse manufacturing sector.

Although 80 percent of the country's total land area is available for farming, only 12 percent is under cultivation because many areas suffer from erratic rainfall, periodic droughts, and soil erosion. Consequently, agriculture only accounts for about 5 percent of the nation's gross domestic product (GDP) and employs one-eighth of the country's workforce. Major agricultural products include corn, wheat, peanuts, sugarcane, grapes, tobacco, and potatoes. South Africa is Africa's most important fishing nation; the oceans surrounding the country's coasts are rich in many fish species, including hake, mackerel, herring, anchovies, pilchards, and rock lobsters.

ENERGY

The country's main source of energy is coal. Most electricity is generated in coal-fired power stations situated near the main coal fields in Gauteng, Free State, and northern KwaZulu Natal. South Africa produces about half the electricity generated in the whole of Africa, but only about half the households in the country have electricity.

Below: These South Africans gather the day's catch from large fishing nets. Today, South Africa's commercial fishing industry employs about twenty-eight thousand people.

Left: This South African miner is drilling for gold in a mine located in Gauteng.

DIAMONDS AND GOLD

The discovery of individual diamonds in 1867 and the gold rush that followed in 1886 started a chain of events that changed the history of South Africa. Fortunes were made and lost as thousands of fortune hunters rushed to strike it rich.

(A Closer Look, page 46)

Mining is, by far, the country's most important industry, and since the end of the nineteenth century, the South African economy has been based on the production and export of its huge mineral reserves. Today, South Africa is the world's largest gold producer, but this industry is facing long-term decline due to its high production costs and falling gold prices. The country also leads the world in the production of gem diamonds and is a major contributor to the world's production of platinum-group metals, uranium, and asbestos. Other chief minerals include coal, iron ore, copper, nickel, and manganese. Apart from gold, South Africa has hardly scratched the surface of its huge mineral deposits, and the country's mining industry is one of the most technologically advanced in the world.

About one-sixth of South Africa's workforce is employed in the manufacturing industry. The country's largest industries are metal products (notably iron and steel), chemicals, food and beverages, electrical machinery, motor vehicles, and textiles. Most of South Africa's manufacturing industries are concentrated in Gauteng, although Durban, Port Elizabeth, and Cape Town are also major industrial cities.

The country's main export trading partners are Switzerland, the United Kingdom, the United States, Japan, and Germany. Imports come mainly from Germany, the United States, the United Kingdom, and Japan.

TRANSPORTATION

The transportation network in South Africa is among the most modern and extensive on the African continent. Railway lines and roads link the country's major cities and towns. Most white South Africans own a car, and the number of car owners among the rest of the population is on the rise. The major ports in Durban, Cape Town, East London, and Port Elizabeth serve the country's shipping needs. The country also has four international airports.

People and Lifestyle

South Africa has a multicultural and multiethnic population. Until 1991, South African law divided its people into four major racial groups: blacks (Africans), whites, coloreds, and Indians. Although this law has been abolished, many South Africans still view themselves and one another according to these categories.

Blacks constitute 75.2 percent of the population, and they belong to four language groups. The Nguni group makes up over half of South Africa's black population and includes various Xhosa, Zulu, Swazi, and Ndebele peoples. Sotho, Pedi, and Tswana peoples form the Sotho-Tswana group. The two other major groups are the Tsonga and the Venda.

Making up 13.6 percent of South Africa's people, whites can be divided into two main groups: Afrikaners and English-speakers. Over three-fifths of the white population are Afrikaners. Afrikaners are descendants of the original Dutch settlers who arrived in South Africa in the 1600s and who were later joined by German and French settlers. The other group consists of English-speakers whose ancestors began to settle in South Africa in large numbers in the nineteenth century.

The coloreds are a mixed race descended primarily from the early European settlers, Malays, and indigenous African peoples.

THE SAN

Believed to be the indigenous people of South Africa, the San still attempt to follow their traditional way of life.
(*A Closer Look, page 58*)

TRADITIONAL MEDICINES

Modern health facilities, such as hospitals and clinics, are scarce in South Africa's rural regions. Many people living in these areas rely on traditional medicines.
(*A Closer Look, page 68*)

Left: **Under the new democratic South Africa, people of all races, including these young girls from Pretoria, can mix freely and form multi-ethnic friendships.**

Today, they represent 8.6 percent of South Africa's population and speak mainly Afrikaans. Forming the largest group in the city of Cape Town, coloreds live mainly in Western Cape, Northern Cape, and Gauteng.

South Africa's Indian community makes up about 2.6 percent of the population. Concentrated in KwaZulu Natal, the Indians are descendants of the Indian workers who were brought to South Africa in the mid-nineteenth century to work the vast sugar plantations in Natal.

More than 95 percent of South African people live in the eastern half of the country, as well as in the southern coastal areas. About half of South Africa's population is urban, including most of the country's whites, Indians, and coloreds. The majority of blacks, however, live in the country's rural areas, although increasing numbers are migrating to the cities in search of work.

SOUTH AFRICA'S MAJOR CITIES

Johannesburg is one of South Africa's major industrial and financial centers. Cape Town is the country's legislative capital, while Pretoria, is the executive capital. Other metropolitan regions are the port city of Durban; Port Elizabeth, a leading industrial area and a major port; and Kimberley, the hub of the country's diamond industry. Although not a city, Soweto, a township located outside of Johannesburg, is one of the largest communities in South Africa.

Family Life

The diverse backgrounds of South Africans have helped create contrasting ways of life. In addition, the inequalities created by the system of apartheid have profoundly affected how South Africans live.

Rural and Township Life

Many black South Africans live in the countryside in areas formerly known as homelands. Here, families tend to be large. Extended families are also common; family members outside the nuclear family often live with the family. Life is extremely difficult in rural South Africa. Because the soil on which the people farm is poor, food is often scarce, and many children die of malnutrition every day. In addition, infant mortality rates are high because medical facilities are not readily available. Unemployment in these areas is very high, at 45 percent, and more than half of the country's rural community lives in poverty.

As a result, many rural black South Africans have moved away from these areas to look for jobs in the cities that will enable them to support their families. Most of these people live in so-called townships on the outskirts of cities and towns. As the number of rural black South Africans flooding into the cities increases, government housing programs struggle to reduce the drastic housing shortages. As a result of insufficient housing,

WOMEN IN THE NEW SOUTH AFRICA

Although laws under the new constitution have drastically improved the opportunities open to women in the labor market, many women still face discrimination daily, especially among South Africa's black ethnic groups.
(A Closer Look, page 70)

HEALTH

Child malnutrition, malaria, tuberculosis, and Acquired Immune Deficiency Syndrome (AIDS) are among the chronic health problems that plague many South Africans. The spread of AIDS in the 1990s had a devastating effect on South Africa. According to U.N. estimates, over 4.2 million adults, or 20 percent of the adult population, had AIDS or the human immuno-deficiency virus (HIV) that leads to AIDS by the end of the decade. As a direct consequence, 700,000 children were orphaned by the disease by 2000.

shantytowns surround the country's major urban areas. These shantytowns consist predominantly of shacks made of cardboard, wood, and corrugated iron. Most of the townships and these squatter settlements lack any basic infrastructure, including access to safe drinking water and facilities such as running water and electricity.

Urban Life

Most white South Africans live in the country's cities and surrounding suburbs. They are westernized and enjoy a high standard of living. White South Africans tend to have small families and live in single-story homes with gardens, often with swimming pools and tennis courts. Wealthy Indians, coloreds, and a small but growing number of black South Africans have lifestyles similar to those of the white population.

People living in the cities are concerned about security because of the high crime rate. The government has set up the Reconstruction and Development Programme (RDP) to address crime and other social problems, such as unemployment.

Below:
Well-to-do families in Johannesburg enjoy modern comforts, such as swimming pools and large gardens.

Education

Education in South Africa is undergoing radical change. Under the apartheid system, schools were segregated according to race, and the quality of education varied significantly across racial groups. Although the laws governing this segregation have been abolished, the long and difficult process of restructuring the country's education system is just beginning. The challenge facing the current government is to create a single nondiscriminatory, nonracial system that offers the same standards of education to all South African people.

Today, all South African children between the ages of seven and fifteen are required to attend school. Almost 99 percent of the children attend one of the country's public, or state, schools. The remaining 1.2 percent attends privately owned, independent schools.

Elementary school lasts for six years and consists of two phases. Junior elementary school, which includes grades one to three, is devoted to reading, writing, mathematics, and language

Below: **This teacher helps two students from Sacred Heart Primary School in Johannesburg with their work. In an attempt to meet the government's targeted forty-to-one pupil-teacher ratio, many black South African children now attend schools in predominantly white areas.**

proficiency. Senior elementary school, grades four to six, includes proficiency in the student's native tongue and a second language, mathematics, history, general science, geography, and a skill, such as needlework, woodwork, or art.

High school also consists of two phases — junior and senior. Junior high school lasts from grade seven through grade nine. Most subjects are compulsory, but students choose two subjects in addition to those required. After grade nine, students may choose to leave school or go on to senior high school for three years. At the end of grade twelve, senior high school students take a public examination on a minimum of six subjects to obtain a Senior Certificate. The Senior Certificate determines whether a student can enter an institute of higher learning.

Higher Education

South Africa currently has twenty-one universities, the oldest and largest of which is the University of South Africa in Pretoria. Established in 1873, the university is one of two South African universities that offers off-site education. Although students from all ethnic groups have been able to attend any of the country's universities since 1994, many still choose a university based on its ethnic history. The nation also has fifteen *technikons* (teck-NEE-cons), or technical institutions, that provide vocational training.

THE SLOW PROCESS OF INTEGRATION

Despite the government's commitment to improving education, the process of integration has been slow. The government is faced with the daunting task of dealing with massive inequalities in teacher qualifications, buildings, sports facilities, and equipment, as well as the sharp contrasts between township schools with relatively good resources and schools in rural areas and shantytowns. Overall, about two thousand new schools need to be built, sixty-five thousand new classrooms equipped, sixty thousand teachers trained, and fifty million textbooks printed.

Religion

South Africa does not have a national religion, although about two-thirds of the population practice some form of Christianity. Another 28.5 percent follows traditional beliefs, while the remainder are Muslim, Hindu, or Jewish.

Christianity

Christianity was introduced to South Africa in the 1600s with the arrival of European settlers. Today, about 68 percent of the population is Christian. Most Afrikaners belong to one of the three Dutch Reformed churches, whose membership of 4.5 million includes half of the country's colored people and a small number of black South Africans. The Dutch Reformed Church, or the Nederduitse Gereformeerde Kerk, is the largest of these three churches and has 4 million members. Most white South Africans who speak English as their first language belong to the Anglican, Methodist, or Roman Catholic churches. Black South Africans are also members of these denominations.

CHURCH AND APARTHEID

Religion in South Africa played a major role in the struggle against apartheid. Religious leaders, such as Archbishop Desmond Tutu and Reverend Allan Boesak, president of the World Alliance of Reformed Churches, became familiar figures on the international stage in their campaigns for equality and democracy in South Africa.

Traditional Beliefs

Before Christianity was brought to South Africa, the country's ethnic groups practiced their own religions. About 28.5 percent of South African people still follow these beliefs. Although these beliefs vary from one group to another, all these traditional religions have certain elements in common. One is the belief in a supreme being. Another element is the worship of spirits, in particular ancestral spirits, that have the power to influence everyday life.

African Initiated Churches

Combining religious practices followed in the West with elements of traditional African religions, African initiated churches began to emerge in South Africa at the end of the nineteenth century. Today, African initiated churches are the fastest growing branch of Christianity in South Africa. The country has over four thousand of these churches, with a collective membership of over 8.5 million. The largest of these churches is the Zion Christian Church, which has about two million followers.

OTHER RELIGIONS

Islam was introduced to South Africa in the seventeenth century by Asian laborers. Today, followers of Islam include half of the country's colored population and a portion of the Indian community. Members of the Indian community also practice Hinduism. South Africa has a Jewish community of approximately 100,000 followers.

Below: **A procession of Zulu worshipers sings during a Zionist church service in Durban.**

Language and Literature

Afrikaans and English used to be the official languages of South Africa. Today, however, the country has eleven official languages, which include nine Bantu languages, to reflect the diversity of its people. The official languages are Afrikaans, English, Ndebele, Pedi, Sotho, Swazi, Tsonga, Tswana, Venda, Xhosa, and Zulu.

Afrikaans evolved from the Dutch spoken by the seventeenth-century settlers, but the language also contains words and phrases from Malay, Portuguese, the Bantu group, Hottentot, and other African languages, as well as from English, French, and German. Afrikaans is the first language of most Afrikaners and colored people. South African English is not much different from the English spoken elsewhere in the world, but it has borrowed many Afrikaans words. English is spoken mainly by white South Africans and most of the Indian community.

Zulu is the most common language among black South Africans. The language contains three types of click sounds that were probably borrowed from speakers of the Khoisan languages. Most Zulu words end in a vowel.

DOMINANT LANGUAGES

The new constitution is very particular about maintaining the right of each South African to speak his or her own language, as well as learn it at school. This right, however, is proving to be difficult to put into practice. English is still the main medium of instruction in schools and most universities, as well as the chief language used in business and industry. Therefore, English and, to a lesser extent, Afrikaans are still the dominant languages in South Africa.

Left: **This street vendor is selling a wide selection of magazines at his stall in Cape Town.**

Literature

South African literature has three main literary traditions in the Bantu, English, and Afrikaans languages. Much of the country's twentieth-century literature reflects political and social tensions within South African society.

The oral tradition among South Africa's black ethnic groups has strongly influenced the written literature of black authors. Favorite themes among writers are tribal history and the conflict between accepting westernization and holding on to traditions. Well-known Zulu writers include poet B. W. Vilakazi (1905–1947). Other authors are Thomas Mofolo (1876–1948), writing in Sotho, and Es'kia Mphahlele (1919–), who produces works in English.

South African literature written in English by white South Africans emerged in 1883 with *The Story of an African Farm* by Olive Schreiner (1855–1920). Since then, many English writers have focused on South Africa's social and political problems. Writers such as Nadine Gordimer (1923–) and Alan Paton (1903–1988) played an important role during the apartheid years, producing works that painted a picture of South Africa for the outside world.

Afrikaner literature was well-developed by the early twentieth century. Early works dealt with the political and linguistic struggles of Afrikaners. Modern writers, such as Breyten Breytenbach (1939–) and André Brink (1935–), have earned international recognition.

LITERATURE AND APARTHEID

During apartheid, the works of many authors were dominated by themes dealing with racial problems and living under an oppressive regime. Many of these works were banned by the South African government, and some authors, such as Breyten Breytenbach, were forced into exile abroad. South African authors who actively opposed apartheid also include Alan Paton, Nadine Gordimer, André Brink, and Athold Fugard (1932–). Probably one of the most famous books to emerge during this period was Paton's *Cry the Beloved Country* (1948), which explores the impact of racism on whites as well as blacks.

Arts

Painting and Sculpture

J. E. A. Volschenk (1853–1936) is considered one of South Africa's first professional artists and is sometimes referred to as the "father of South African art." His landscape paintings were influenced by the artistic traditions of the Netherlands and Britain. Later artists, such as Hugo Naudé (1869–1941), broke away from the traditional style of painting, which featured romantic landscapes, and began to portray the South African landscape as it really is.

The traditional form of black South African art is the mural, or wall painting. Some of the best mural art has been produced by the Ndebele tribe, who use bold and brightly colored patterns to decorate their homes. Modern art of black South Africans originated in the townships around Johannesburg in the 1950s. Known as "township art," this type of art reflected the struggles of black South Africans under the system of apartheid.

South Africa has also produced some prominent sculptors, such as Anton van Wouw (1862–1945), who is best known for his monuments, and Coert Laurens Steynberg (1905–1982).

ROCK ART: A SACRED HERITAGE

The most ancient art to be found in South Africa is that of the San. Dating from the Stone Age, the San painted scenes of family life, hunting, and fighting on rocks and on the walls of caves all over the country, notably in the mountain regions.
(A Closer Look, page 56)

Below: Colorful murals, such as this one in Durban, are either painted on the sides of houses or on walls. These murals liven up bleak neighborhoods and usually show scenes that celebrate life.

Left: **Dressed in traditional costume, a group of Zulus sings to the beat of traditional Zulu percussion instruments in front of a crowd of onlookers in the streets of Johannesburg.**

RICH MUSICAL TRADITIONS

Through the unique musical styles of Zensi Miriam Makeba and Hugh Masekela and the groundbreaking work of Juluka and Ladysmith Black Mambazo, millions of people around the world have been introduced to the diverse sounds of South African music.
(A Closer Look, page 54)

Music

Black South Africans have an ancient musical tradition, and music is an important element of tribal life, particularly in ceremonies and rituals. African traditional music is either sung or played on instruments, such as drums, animal horns, stringed instruments derived from the shooting bow, and xylophones. One type of traditional tribal music that has become popular throughout South Africa and abroad is *iscathamiya* (is-COT-ah-me-yah), which is traditional Zulu call-and-response choral music sung without instrumental accompaniment.

Many forms of South African music have developed over the decades and reflect a combination of traditional music, especially of the Zulu and Sotho peoples, with African-American rhythm and blues and jazz. *Mbaqanga* (um-bah-TZAN-gah), which developed in the segregated black townships created under apartheid, is a popular form of dance music.

South Africa also has a number of symphony orchestras. Among the country's most well-known composers are Arnold van Wyk (1916–1983), Hubert du Plessis (1922–), and John Joubert (1927–), all of whom have contributed to international classical music.

MBAQANGA AND KWAITO

Present on South Africa's music scene for a number of decades, mbaqanga draws on American jazz, soul music, Afro rock, local *kwela* (KWEH-lah), or street music, and the choral music of rural African communities. The latest type of music to come out of urban black areas is *kwaito* (KWEH-toh). Extremely popular with today's youth, this type of music remixes international recordings to give them local feeling by slowing down the speed and adding percussion and African melodies.

31

Architecture

South Africa has a rich and varied architectural heritage, to which all of its cultural groups have contributed. Throughout the centuries, the country's African ethnic groups have built different types of mud and grass huts. The most easily recognizable of these are the beehive-shaped huts of the Zulus. Known as *kraals* (KRAHLS), these huts are made of straw and have only one opening that serves as a doorway.

The country, however, is probably best known for its distinctive Cape Dutch buildings, found mainly in Western Cape. Considered one of the world's most beautiful types of domestic architecture, this style developed in the 1600s and 1700s and featured thick, whitewashed walls, steep roofs, curved gables, and long, raised verandas.

In the nineteenth century, South African architecture was predominantly British Colonial in a variety of revival styles, such as Gothic and neoclassical. Twentieth-century South African architecture was heavily influenced by Sir Herbert Baker (1862–1946), who designed the Union Buildings in Pretoria and Saint George's Cathedral in Cape Town.

Above: **Believed to have been built around 1685 as part of a large estate, Groot Constantia, located in Cape Town, is the oldest building in Western Cape and is a magnificent example of Cape Dutch architecture.**

Handicrafts

South Africa is famous for its tribal handicrafts. The country's various African ethnic groups, such as the Zulus, Ndebele, Sotho, and Xhosa, produce an amazing variety of wonderful carvings, statues, beadwork, and basketry.

Beautiful carvings and statues are made of wood or stone. Common themes are giraffes and rhinoceroses, as well as graceful women carrying loads on their heads. Artists also carve everyday objects, such as spoons, bowls, and pots. Using locally available cane, reed, bark, and palm leaves, women make mats and weave baskets and colorful carpets. Ndebele and Zulu women are also known for their elaborate beadwork.

Dance

Dance has many forms in South Africa, ranging from tribal dance to modern dance and ballet. Ethnic groups have their own special dance styles, such as those of young Zulu and Ndebele men who recall the victories of past warriors. During the apartheid years, protest musicals performed in the theater brought about distinctive dancing styles, such as the *toyi-toyi* (TOY-TOY), a militant marching dance adapted from protest marches and traditional Zulu dances. Classical ballet is also popular in South Africa, and the country is home to two professional companies based in Pretoria and Cape Town.

ZULU BEADWORK

The women of the Zulu ethnic group are world famous for their beadwork (*above*), which is admired for its intricate designs and its mysterious color-coded message system.
(*A Closer Look, page 72*)

Left: **These beautiful handwoven baskets and carved wooden masks are on sale at a market in Cape Town. Traditional handicrafts are also sold along roads linking major towns and in up-market curio shops. In addition, the country's booming tourist industry has turned some craft-making into small businesses.**

Leisure and Festivals

In rural areas, South Africans must work hard to earn a living, either by farming or by selling fruits, vegetables, or arts and crafts. This work leaves them with very little free time. Consequently, for many people in rural communities, social interaction is built into work. Women often perform household chores together, such as washing or cooking, so they can chat and exchange news. They also enjoy doing crafts, such as embroidery, basketry, and beadwork. Children play soccer and like to make objects out of basic materials, such as bottle tops and old tin cans.

Relaxing in Urban South Africa

In cities, residents enjoy a wide range of pastimes. People go to theaters, live shows, and the movies, as well as visit the country's numerous museums and art galleries. South Africans also like to meet friends at restaurants, coffee shops, and tea gardens to catch up on the latest news. Young South Africans enjoy window shopping and often spend their evenings at discos.

MAGNIFICENT ARTWORK OF THE NDEBELE WOMEN

While lamp posts, car registration numbers, and telephone poles are part of everyday life for most people, these objects provide the Ndebele women with inspiration for bold designs for wall paintings and beadwork.
(A Closer Look, page 48)

Below: **These young boys in Eastern Cape are having fun playing with old car tires.**

SHEBEEN

The *shebeen* (shah-BEEN), or public house, is where urban black South Africans socialize in the evenings. A shebeen is often crowded with people drinking home-made brews and other types of beverages. Shebeens started to emerge in South Africa's townships during apartheid. For many years, shebeens were illegal, as the sale of liquor was subject to strict laws that required a license. Today, shebeens are popular places to relax.

Many South Africans who live in the suburbs like entertaining informally at home in the garden. This type of entertaining usually centers around a *braaivleis* (BREYE-flace), or barbecue.

The Great Outdoors

City residents who want to escape city life take short drives to the many nearby parks and game reserves to participate in many popular outdoor activities, such as hiking, camping, bird-watching, and fishing. Walking is also a favorite pastime, and South Africans explore the country's veld, wilderness, and coastal shorelines on a network of marked trails. Special trails cater to people who are interested in bird-watching, game viewing, or examining South African vegetation. Other popular leisure activities are white-water rafting, canoeing, bungee jumping, cycling, jogging, and marathon running.

With 1,739 miles (2,798 km) of coastline, South Africa offers unlimited water sports, including sailing, water skiing, surfing, and scuba diving. More common activities are swimming, sunbathing, and fishing.

OUTDOOR CONCERTS

Botanical gardens and parks throughout the country provide a scenic backdrop for outdoor musical concerts and performances, ranging from jazz to classical music. South Africans enjoy gathering for these performances and usually bring a picnic, as well as blankets for comfortable seating.

Sports

South Africans are passionate about sports. The country's mild climate enables South Africans to spend much of their leisure time outdoors participating in or watching one of the many sports they enjoy. For a long time, however, South Africa's sports teams were not allowed to compete in overseas tournaments due to an international sports boycott of South Africa. By 1992, the sports ban had been lifted. Since then, South African sportsmen and women have been welcomed back into the international sports arena.

South African children participate in a large variety of sports, including volleyball, hockey, tennis, track and field events, and swimming. Boys also enjoy rugby, soccer, and cricket, while many girls play netball. Favorite spectator sports among South African adults are soccer, rugby, track and field, tennis, and cricket.

Soccer is the most popular sport among black South Africans. Over thirty thousand soccer clubs provide facilities for the country's soccer players, who number 1.2 million. Of this figure, the majority of players are black. Popular soccer teams that compete in the country's Premier Soccer League (PSL) are the Orlando Pirates, the Mamelodi Sundowns, and the Kaizer Chiefs.

Rugby is also a favorite sport, especially among Afrikaners. Competitions are played at local, provincial, and national levels. The country's top teams participate in the annual Tri-Nations

BAFANA BAFANA

South Africa's national soccer team, affectionately known as Bafana Bafana, competes regularly in international events. Since returning to international soccer in 1992, the team has been victorious in the African Cup of Nations, which it won in 1996. The team also qualified for the 1998 World Cup championship held in France. In June 2001, the Fédération Internationale de Football Association (FIFA), the world body governing soccer, ranked Bafana Bafana twenty-fourth in the world.

Below: Soccer is very popular in South Africa, and amateur teams throughout the country participate in various leagues and competitions.

Left: A rugby player attempts to make his way to the opponent's goal area to score a try while playing in a match in Durban. Rugby was brought to South Africa by British settlers in the nineteenth century. Today, the sport is played throughout the country.

Series, which includes the Southern Hemisphere powerhouses of New Zealand, Australia, and South Africa. The South African team won this prestigious competition in 1998. The national rugby team has also performed well since rejoining the international rugby scene in 1995. In that year, South Africa hosted and won the Rugby World Cup after beating New Zealand in the finals.

Track and field also has a huge following, and the country has produced some world-class long-distance runners, such as Josia Thugwane, Hendrick Ramaala, Lucas Matlala, and Colin Thomas. South Africa is best known for the Comrades Marathon. Held annually in June, the event tests the stamina of all participants who run a grueling 54-mile (86.7-km) route between Durban and Pietermaritzburg. Another popular ultramarathon, or footrace that is longer than a marathon, is Cape Town's Two Oceans Marathon.

A new generation of tennis players has emerged recently from South Africa, most notably Amanda Coetzer and Wayne Ferreira. The international success of these players has helped promote the sport among the South African population.

Despite growing interest among black South Africans, cricket is still largely followed by white South Africans. The sport is played at all levels. South Africa will host the Cricket World Cup in 2003.

JOSIA THUGWANE

Earning instant fame in his sports-crazy home-land, Josia Thugwane (*below*) became the first black South African to win an Olympic gold medal at the 1996 Olympic Games, held in Atlanta, United States. A year later, Thugwane broke the South African national marathon record in Fukuoka, Japan, with a time of 2 hours, 7 minutes, and 28 seconds.

Left: **Apart from the country's national holidays, South Africans celebrate other holidays, such as New Year's Day, with colorful parades through the streets of major cities, including Cape Town.**

Festivals

Many holidays celebrated during the years of apartheid are no longer recognized in the new constitution. They have been replaced by new holidays that recognize the cultures of the country's diverse ethnic groups.

National Holidays

Today, South Africa's national holidays reflect the country's historical struggle for the political freedom of its people and its dedication to the basic human rights of all South Africans. Human Rights' Day on March 21 honors protestors who were killed by authorities during a demonstration in Sharpeville in 1960. Freedom Day on April 27 marks the anniversary of the first free elections held in South Africa in 1994. Youth Day takes place on June 16 and is a day of remembrance for students who were killed by police in Soweto on that day in 1976. South African women are honored on National Women's Day on August 9 for their participation in the resistance to apartheid. December 16 was formerly known as the Day of the Vow, a national holiday that commemorated the defeat of the Zulus by Boer forces at the Battle of Blood River in 1838. Today, the holiday is known as the Day of Reconciliation and encourages all South Africans to come together to create a new, unified country.

THE NATIONAL ARTS FESTIVAL

The biggest celebration of the country's rich cultural heritage is the National Arts Festival, held annually in Grahamstown. Every imaginable art form is represented at this diverse festival, from theater to dance, opera to cabaret, fine art to craft art, classical music to jazz, and poetry readings to lectures. The festival also includes medieval banquets, techno raves, craft fairs, cyber cafés, carnivals, street musicians, and walking tours.

Traditional Festivals

South Africa's tribal peoples have numerous traditional festivals. Most of these festivals center around major events in an individual's life, such as birth, circumcision, or marriage. Initiation, one of the most important events, marks a child's passage into adulthood. Among the Xhosa, initiation for a boy is characterized by a period of isolation, in which he undergoes training and endurance tests. During this time, the boy shaves his head, wears special clothing, and smears his body from head to toe with white clay. At the end of this period, the boy is circumcised. He then returns to his village and is covered in red clay, which is not removed for another three months. After this period, the boy is considered a man.

Religious Holidays

Christian holy days, such as Christmas Day and Good Friday, are national holidays. On Christmas Day, many South African families go to church. They then return home to exchange gifts and eat a large meal together. The country's Jews, Hindus, and Muslims also observe their traditional holy days.

Above: **The initiation of this Xhosa boy in KwaZulu Natal marks his transition from child to adult. The white blanket with red bands is part of the special clothing that a Xhosa boy wears during this time.**

Left: **Besides recognizing South Africa's national holidays, Zulus also annually celebrate Shaka's Day in September. This holiday is marked by celebrations to commemorate the founder of the Zulu kingdom. On this day, Zulus wear full traditional attire and gather at Shaka's tombstone in Stanger, KwaZulu Natal.**

Food

South Africa's rich historical and cultural heritage has produced a cuisine that has African, Dutch, English, French, German, Afrikaner, Malay, and Indian influences.

Traditional African food tends to be simple. The basis of most meals is *pap* (PUP), or cornmeal porridge, which can be eaten for breakfast with milk or sour milk and sugar. It can also be served as a main dish with a savory sauce or in a tomato and onion stew with barbecued or stewed meat or chicken. A favorite dish is *umngqusho* (um-tzuh-GOO-show), which is made from corn kernels, sugar beans, butter, onions, potatoes, chili, and lemons. Stews are made from a variety of plants, such as blackjack, purslane, and pigweed, while insects and mopani worms serve as an excellent source of protein.

Cape Malay dishes are characterized by sweet, aromatic curries. *Bobotie* (ber-BOW-ah-tee) is a baked dish made with minced beef or lamb, onions, curry powder, tumeric, and lemons. It is usually served with yellow rice and condiments. *Bredies*

Below: These young children in Soweto are eating a meal of pap and different types of vegetables.

(BREAR-dees) are stews made from any type of meat and various kinds of vegetables. *Waterblommetjie bredie* (VAH-ter-bloh-mer-key BREAR-dee), made from waterlilies that grow only in Western Cape, is extremely popular and a truly unique South African dish. Like Cape Malay food, Indian dishes contain many spices and curried flavors. One favorite dish is *breyani* (bray-AH-nee), a spicy rice dish made with lentils, other vegetables, and fish, chicken, or mutton.

Afrikaner cuisine has many remnants of the trekking days. The braaivleis originated with the trekkers and is still very popular today. An essential ingredient of any braaivleis is *boerewors* (BOO-er-vors), or sausage made of beef, mutton, or venison and seasoned with various spices. Chops, steaks, and *sosaties* (soh-SAH-tees), or marinated kabobs, are often served with pap, salads, and baked potatoes. Most Afrikaner meals consist of one or more types of meat, including beef, Karoo lamb, springbok, or other game, and vegetables, such as sweet potatoes and pumpkins. Snacks include *biltong* (bill-TONG), or dried strips of meat, such as beef or venison, that are soaked in salt. Popular cakes and pastries include *koeksuster* (COOK-sis-ter), a twisted doughnut fried in oil and covered in syrup, and *melktert* (MELK-tairt), a cinnamon-flavored custard tart.

Above: **A traditional staple food, pap with tomato-based gravy is a favorite lunchtime meal among black South Africans.**

Below: **Wine-making in South Africa began after 1652 when Dutch settlers realized the climate in present-day Western Cape was ideal for growing grapes. Today, the country is home to numerous wineries that produce exquisite, world-class wines.**

A CLOSER LOOK AT SOUTH AFRICA

Throughout most of the twentieth century, South Africa made international headlines because of the government's system of apartheid and the incarceration of the world's most famous political prisoner, Nelson Mandela. Even before then, the country had experienced a colorful but turbulent past as tribal chiefs, such as Shaka, fought for domination, and European settlers battled for control of the country's fantastic mineral wealth.

Throughout the centuries, South Africans have shown courage and determination to keep their traditions alive. Much of the nation's rich tribal heritage survives to this day, including the

Opposite: **Wrapped in a blanket characteristic of her tribe, a Ndebele woman threads colorful beads to make a beautiful neckband.**

ancient rock art of the San and the art- and beadwork of the Ndebele and Zulu tribes. Many South African performers have fused their musical traditions with modern trends to produce unique musical sounds that are appreciated the world over.

With tourism on the rise, many people are now discovering firsthand the natural beauty of South Africa. Constantly aware of its responsibility toward the animal kingdom, the country has implemented conservation efforts to protect the many precious and often indigenous plants and animals that make their homes throughout South Africa and in its surrounding seas.

Above: **This solitary fisherman enjoys the peace and quiet of the coast along northern KwaZulu Natal.**

Conservation

Ever since rampant hunting by European settlers and the establishment and expansion of settlements led to the near extinction of many animals and indigenous plant life, conservation has been a vital issue in South Africa. As early as the 1880s, farsighted people began to make provisions to protect the country's enormous variety of plant and animal species. Despite political and social upheaval in the country during the twentieth century, this legacy has continued, and, today, South Africa is a world leader in the field of wildlife conservation.

Through this concerted effort to conserve the nation's biodiversity, extensive parks and nature reserves have been set up throughout the country. These protected areas now cover roughly 5.5 percent of the country's surface area, and approximately 74 percent of plants, 92 percent of amphibians, 92 percent of reptiles, 97 percent of birds, and 93 percent of mammals in South Africa are represented in these specially designated regions.

Above: **Dehorning the country's remaining rhinoceroses is just one measure South African conservationists are taking in an attempt to save the species from falling prey to illegal hunting.**

WILDLIFE-BASED TOURISM

South Africa is home to many privately owned parks and nature reserves that have produced successful wildlife-based tourism enterprises. These parks not only enable tourists to stay in areas where wildlife lives naturally but also increase the survival rate of individual species. In addition, this type of tourism benefits local communities as it provides both jobs and sources of income for residents of the area.

Left: **The impala is just one of many animals that make their home in the wilds of South Africa.**

Left: **Zebras and a herd of elephants congregate at one of the watering holes in Kruger National Park. In South Africa, protecting the country's animal and plant life goes hand in hand with protecting the environment in which these species live. These habitats are gradually being destroyed by pollution, urbanization, and overutilization by the human population.**

Success Stories

Vigilant efforts of the various nature conservation authorities and individual wildlife organizations have contributed greatly toward the spectacular recovery of certain species from the brink of extinction. Conservation successes include an increase in the number of common animals, including impalas, zebras, and gemsboks, as well as rare animal species, such as the white rhinoceros and the elephant. The country is also at the forefront of captive breeding programs for endangered species, such as the cheetah and wild dog.

Combating Illegal Trade

Many of South Africa's animal and plant species are tempting targets for illegal exploitation because collectors are willing to pay high prices to own rare wildlife products. Ironically, South Africa's well-developed infrastructure of roads, railways, and air traffic contributes to the ease of smuggling these illegal products out of the country. Supported by wildlife organizations, the South African government is trying to combat this illegal trade by implementing harsh laws, such as heavy fines and imprisonment, for those caught smuggling endangered species or illegal wildlife products out of the country.

CAPE FLORISTIC REGION

South Africa is the only country in the world to have an entire plant kingdom within its borders. Also known as the Fynbos Region, the Cape Floristic Region is recognized internationally for its unique plant life. Containing nine thousand plant species, six thousand of which are found nowhere else on Earth, this region is the most threatened of the world's six floral kingdoms. Threats to the future of this area come from agriculture, soil erosion, urbanization, pollution, and poaching. Fourteen hundred plant species are now rare, endangered, or close to extinction.

Diamonds and Gold

The discovery of diamonds and gold in South Africa in the nineteenth century not only began the country's transformation from an agricultural economy into an industrialized nation but also shaped the social fabric of twentieth-century South Africa.

South Africa's diamond rush began in 1867 when a stone found near the Orange River was identified as a 21-carat diamond. Other diamonds were found along the Orange, Vaal, and Harts rivers later that year, and a large-scale diamond rush followed. By the end of 1871, nearly fifty thousand people were living in a thriving, sprawling mining town that was named Kimberley in 1873. The South African countryside underwent a radical transformation as railways were built, infrastructure was developed, and commerce was encouraged.

Farther north, a 40-mile (64-km) belt of gold-bearing deposits was discovered on the Witwatersrand in 1886. These deposits, or reefs, turned out to be the richest gold fields in the world and led to the establishment of the city of Johannesburg. Within three years, Johannesburg became the largest city in the country as fortune hunters flocked there by the tens of thousands.

THE BIG HOLE

Located near Kimberley, the Kimberley Mine (*above*), or the "Big Hole," is the largest hand-dug diamond mine in the world. As diggers went deeper and deeper into the ground in search of diamonds, many claims collapsed into one another, eventually forming the Big Hole. Mined to a depth of 705 feet (215 m), the Big Hole produced 14,504,566 diamonds from 22.5 million tons (20,412,000 metric tonnes) of earth by the time the mine was closed in 1914.

Left: European and African laborers working in one of the first gold mines established on the Witwatersrand pose for a photo taken at the end of the nineteenth century.

At first, people of all races individually worked small stakes by hand for both diamonds and gold. As the extent of the mineral wealth became apparent, however, mining capitalists bought out individual diggers, and big corporations took control.

The First Steps toward Racial Segregation

The mining magnates centralized and mechanized production in both the diamond and gold mines. They also adopted measures to maximize profits and reduce labor costs. Regulations regarding labor recruitment, wages, and accommodations were based strictly along racial lines and laid the foundations for a future South African society based on racial inequality.

The ratio of white to black workers was strictly controlled. Furthermore, white gold miners were able to earn high wages, earning nine times as much as their black counterparts, because of their skills, scarcity, and political power. Likewise in the diamond mines, white diggers employed as skilled workers or overseers demanded high wages, while the workforce consisted mainly of unskilled, low-paid African migrant workers.

Finally, as African workers left their homes and came from all over the country and beyond to work, they were housed in segregated, fenced-off compounds. Mining companies were able to reduce overhead costs by keeping migrant wages as low as possible.

FROM RURAL LIFE TO LIFE IN THE MINES

The diamond and gold mines profoundly affected the lives of South African people. The ever-increasing need for labor in the mines attracted thousands of people from rural areas. Young African men eager to gain financial independence and earn enough money to pay a bride price left their homes to work in the mines. Those who returned to their homes told stories about the mines, which encouraged even more young men to try their luck.

Magnificent Artwork of the Ndebele Women

The wall paintings and beadwork created by the women of the Ndebele are striking cultural markers that make Ndebele artwork distinct from other South African tribal art.

The Ndebele artistic tradition is passed from mother to daughter, but the women seem to be born with an innate urge to express themselves in design and color. Ndebele women are very creative in their art. Walls are painted freehand, using only the fingers. Although the women now use modern acrylic paints, they traditionally used paints made from natural materials, such as clay and ash, to create uncomplicated triangular and V-shaped designs. Soon, designs became increasingly elaborate, and, by the 1950s, wall patterns began to show urban and Western influences.

Today, Ndebele women draw their inspiration for shapes and designs from everyday life. Letters from the alphabet, such as "N"

ARTISTIC STROKES

Using brightly colored patterns, Ndebele women decorate entire walls on the exterior and interior of their houses. Although the painting surfaces may vary in shape and size, the painting process does not. First, the women create the geometric patterns by drawing a black outline of the design on a white wall surface. Then, they fill in the various parts of the design with green, pink, blue, yellow, red, purple, and other colors.

Left: **Dressed in bright clothing, this Ndebele woman sits proudly in front of her artwork, which decorates the side of her house located in a village outside of Pretoria.**

for Ndebele, are featured in their normal form or are elaborated for design effect. Telephone poles, lamp posts, airplanes, and the symmetrical, geometric patterns of razor blades also provide inspiration. Motifs from nature, such as wheat, are common and are thought to express the hope of a good harvest. Circles are often employed, too. The most common theme, however, is that of the house and items relating to the home, including steps, rooflines, and even light fixtures.

Ndebele Beadwork

Beadwork is also an integral part of Ndebele life and forms an essential part of female garments. Ndebele beadwork is similar to wall paintings in color and design. Beadwork is worn on the head, neck, waist, arms, and legs. Beads are also sewn on goatskins and canvas and worn as aprons. Beaded necklaces and arm and neck rings form part of an outfit that is worn during rituals, such as initiations and weddings.

THE NDEBELE FOUNDATION

Founded in 1996, the Ndebele Foundation was set up to conserve the paint and beadwork skills of the Ndebele women and to create job opportunities. The foundation has established a school where girls can learn beading and painting. The school also aims to provide a sales outlet for Ndebele women to sell their artwork.

Nelson Mandela

Nelson Mandela is South Africa's greatest hero. He is greatly admired all over the world for his dignity, courage, humility, and respect for humankind and has become a legend in his own time.

Born in 1918 to the chief of the Thembu people, Nelson Rolihlahla Mandela renounced his claim to the chieftainship to become a lawyer. In 1944, Mandela joined the Youth League of the ANC, a black liberation group that aimed to eliminate apartheid and achieve equal rights for all South Africans.

Mandela soon became a prominent figure in the ANC. He helped revitalize the party and took part in nonviolent protests, strikes, and marches. The ANC's peaceful attempt to end apartheid ended in 1960, when the ANC was banned following the Sharpeville Massacre, in which at least sixty-seven black demonstrators were killed by police. Consequently, Mandela abandoned his nonviolent policy and called for acts of sabotage against the South African government. Enlisting support for the ANC from abroad, Mandela went underground for more than a year and earned the nickname the "Black Pimpernel."

In 1962, Mandela was arrested and sentenced to five years in prison. While he was in prison, police raided the headquarters of the military wing of the ANC and discovered large quantities of arms and equipment. The imprisoned Mandela and several other ANC members were tried for sabotage, treason, and violent conspiracy in the Rivonia Trial. On June 12, 1964, Mandela was sentenced to life imprisonment.

Mandela was jailed on Robben Island, off Cape Town, from 1964 to 1982 and then at Pollsmoor Prison until 1988, when he was hospitalized. Despite his incarceration, Mandela had wide support among black South Africans, and the struggle against apartheid continued and intensified.

After twenty-seven years in prison, Mandela was released on February 11, 1990. Along with President F. W. de Klerk, Mandela played a key role in South Africa's transition from an apartheid state to a democratic nation. His dream of a free democracy, for which he had fought and sacrificed his youth and personal freedom, finally came true when he became South Africa's first black president on May 10, 1994.

Above: This photo of Nelson Mandela was taken in 1961. As a young man, Mandela worked as a lawyer. Years of daily exposure to the injustices of apartheid led him to seek ways to improve the plight of black South Africans. As a result, he joined the ANC in 1944.

Opposite: Nelson Mandela addresses the press at a conference held shortly after his release in 1990. Over the following four years, Mandela and President F. W. de Klerk worked together to end apartheid and bring about a peaceful transition to a non-racial democracy in South Africa. In 1993, they were awarded the Nobel Prize for Peace for their efforts.

The Mystery of the Cape of Good Hope

The first European to set eyes on what is now known as the Cape of Good Hope was a Portuguese navigator named Bartholomeu Dias. Born c. 1450, Dias is considered one of Portugal's greatest navigators and explorers. Working for the Portuguese crown, Dias set sail in 1487 to ascertain the southern limit of the African continent. During his voyage, he sighted and rounded the cape the following year, opening the sea route to Asia via the Atlantic and Indian Oceans. One historical account says Dias named the cape "Cape of Storms" because the seas around the cape were so stormy and rough. Upon Dias's return to Portugal, however, the Portuguese king, John II, changed the name to "Cape of Good Hope" because of the commercial importance of the new route to the East. Other sources attribute the present name to Dias himself. Tragically, Dias was lost at sea around the Cape of Good Hope in 1500, thus perishing in the very waters he had been the first to navigate.

Known since then for its stormy weather and rough seas, the treacherous rocks and reefs around the Cape of Good Hope have wrecked many ships over the centuries, giving rise to stories and alleged sightings of phantom ships.

Opposite: **The Cape of Good Hope is often regarded as the extremity of the African continent. Contrary to common belief, however, Cape L'Agulhas, to the southeast, is actually the southernmost point of Africa.**

Below: **Known for its natural beauty and breathtaking views, the Cape of Good Hope has also been the site of many shipwrecks since Bartholomeu Dias first sailed around it in 1488.**

The Wild Coast on the Indian Ocean has also been the scene of tragic shipwrecks. In 1552, a Portuguese ship called *Sao Joao* ran aground on the rocks of the coast. Four hundred and forty survivors set out on a grueling journey of 994 miles (1,600 km) to a Portuguese settlement in Mozambique. Only twenty-five people eventually reached safety.

In August 1782, the ill-fated *Grosvenor* was battered on the Wild Coast's treacherous rocks and sank. Between 139 and 153 people were on board, and more than one hundred survived the wreck. Only eight people, however, survived the 117-day trek to Cape Town. Since then, many fortune hunters have tried to locate the wreck and its treasure of diamonds and gems. Lives and fortunes have been lost in the attempts. In April 2000, however, a Hungarian archaeologist finally located the wreck of the *Grosvenor*. Although a number of artifacts have been found to date, the treasure itself is yet to be discovered.

Phantom Ships and Shipwrecks

One of the cape's most famous phantom ships is *The Flying Dutchman*. Legend has it that a Dutch captain named Hendrik van der Decken attempted to sail his ship, *The Flying Dutchman*, through the dangerous waters around the cape during a terrible storm in the early seventeenth century. Unable to withstand the weather, the ship crashed into the rocks at Cape Point. Although the mast had been smashed and the sails were in tatters, the captain vowed to sail around the cape, even if it took him until doomsday. His vow became a prophecy, and, ever since, people claim to have seen *The Flying Dutchman* foundering on the rocks around the cape.

Shipwrecks around the Cape of Good Hope have not been just in the distant past. In 1966, the S. A. *Seafarer*, laden with deadly chemical goods, struck the rocks a few hundred yards (m) from land, showing that even modern instruments and radar are no match for these treacherous waters. The possibility of a poisonous gas leak or of fire terrified all on board as the ship began to sink slowly. Although land was close by, the coast guard was not able to send out lifeboats, as the boats were unable to weather the seas. Had it not been for the modern convenience of a helicopter rescue, these seamen would have met the same fate as many others before them.

Rich Musical Traditions

South African musicians and singers have enriched the world music scene with the rhythm and power of their tribal heritage. Many of the country's greatest musicians and bands kept alive musical traditions that were curbed during the apartheid years. Today, these and younger South African musicians continue to influence musical trends around the world.

A Living Legend

One of the first black South African artists to gain international acclaim was Hugh Masekela. Credited with creating a new type of music by combining African music with pop and jazz, Masekela began his career playing trumpet with various local jazz bands. An outspoken opponent of apartheid, Masekela lived in exile, making his home in the United States, Europe, and other African countries, while bringing his own country's unique rhythms and harmonies to international stages. After almost thirty years in exile, Masekela returned to South Africa in 1990, where he continues to be one of the leading figures in South African music.

Left: Hugh Masekela is a world-famous trumpeter. While in exile, Masekela studied at the Royal Academy of Music and the Manhattan School of Music in New York. Throughout his career, he has tirelessly toured and recorded, becoming one of South Africa's most noted cultural ambassadors.

Left (left to right):
Zensi Miriam Makeba, Ray Phiri, Paul Simon, and Hugh Masekela posed for a group photo in London before they embarked on a worldwide tour promoting Simon's *Graceland* album.

"World Beat"

Creating hybrid music styles by injecting Western music with African rhythm and beat is at the heart of South African music today. Inspiring many great artists, including Paul Simon and Peter Gabriel, this fusion of African and Western styles has become known as "world beat."

Johnny Clegg was instrumental in popularizing this musical style. His fascination with African music began when he heard the street musician Mntonganazo Mzila. He subsequently spent two years learning the basics of Zulu music and dance before forming Juluka, South Africa's first multiethnic band, in the late 1970s. Formed during the height of the struggle against apartheid, this multicultural group served as a powerful symbol of unity and equality. Despite strict apartheid laws that limited where the band could perform, Juluka went on to record two platinum and five gold albums.

Another band that is synonymous with world beat music is Ladysmith Black Mambazo. Founded by Joseph Shabalala, the band's unique style is based on iscathamiya, or Zulu harmony singing. The powerful bass, alto, and tenor voices of Ladysmith Black Mambazo have established the band as the number one recording group in Africa.

GRACELAND

Many people around the world were first introduced to South African music with the release of Paul Simon's *Graceland* album in 1986. Simon collaborated with some of South Africa's finest musicians, such as Hugh Masekela, Miriam Makeba, and Ladysmith Black Mambazo, to produce an album that mixed Western music trends with traditional South African music. These musicians also toured with Simon on the subsequent *Graceland* tour despite international criticism that the tour violated both the ANC's cultural boycott and international sanctions against South Africa.

Rock Art: A Sacred Heritage

South Africa has one of the richest heritages of rock art in the world. Drawn by the San, who first roamed southern Africa thousands of years ago, rock art can be found in caves and shelters formed by overhanging rocks, as well as on hidden rocky outcrops. The art form, which includes paintings and engravings, is testimony to the tribe's culture, religion, and way of life.

The country's mountain regions, especially the Drakensberg Mountains, are home to the most fascinating rock art paintings. Rock engravings are scattered throughout the interior of South Africa on flat rock surfaces.

Archaeologists and art historians believe rock paintings were produced in many ways, using fingers, animal hair brushes, sticks, or feathers. The painters used pigments made from natural resources. Red, orange, and purple were made from lumps of heated iron oxides. White paint was made from fine clay, and manganese oxide or burned bone was used to produce black. The artists often painted over earlier images or made additions to existing ones. They also incorporated natural features, such as cracks on the rock surface, into their

Left: Many San paintings are visual representations of the spirit world. These figures found in Free State depict a shaman and his followers dancing around a fire.

ROCK ART RESEARCH INSTITUTE

The Rock Art Research Institute (RARI) at the University of the Witwatersrand is dedicated to the study, preservation, and promotion of South Africa's rock art. With more than fifteen thousand known rock art sites in the country, the RARI investigates, records, and explains the art so it can be enjoyed by people throughout the world.

paintings. In contrast, the majority of rock engravings were made by scratching or wearing down rock surfaces with stone tools.

The San used rock art to record spiritual, ritual, and day-to-day experiences. Life for the San was (and still is) interconnected with the spirit world. The link between the real world and the spirit world was the shaman, or medicine man, who went into a trance to draw on supernatural powers to cure illness, prevent danger, attract game, or call for rain. In order to share his experiences in the spirit world with the community, the shaman painted the events on rock faces. Other rock art depicted themes of a hunter-gatherer existence.

Later paintings and engravings became an expression of the San trying to come to terms with the radical changes in their world. Interaction with newcomers, such as Bantu-speaking groups and Europeans, encroaching on their living space was increasingly recorded. So too was the fighting that broke out between the groups. Bantu people were shown with spears and cattle, while European settlers were drawn on horseback with rifles. As the new settlers pushed the San farther into semidry areas, fewer paintings and engravings were made. The San's rock-art tradition stopped altogether in the nineteenth century.

Below: This beautiful detail of a San rock painting in the Drakensberg Mountains shows a herd of antelope.

The San

The San, a hunter-gatherer people, were probably the first inhabitants of South Africa. Moving from place to place according to the season and the availability of game, the San lived successfully in even the driest and wettest areas of the region.

Between the eighteenth and early twentieth centuries, the San experienced major changes in their way of life due to the European colonization of southern Africa. Many were killed while fighting Europeans and other African peoples for the control of natural resources. These natural resources were essential for the San to be able to continue their hunting and gathering way of life. Some San died from diseases, such as smallpox, that were introduced by the colonists. Others were drawn into colonial society as domestic servants, farm laborers, or industrial workers.

Although most of the surviving San have been restricted by European settlement or forced by other tribal Africans to semidry areas, San culture still exists today in the northwestern part of the country.

WHY ARE THE BUSHMEN NOW CALLED THE SAN?

Early Dutch settlers began to refer to the San (*above*) as Bushmen in the seventeenth century. At first, the term simply referred to the ethnic group's different way of life, but the term took on a racial meaning in the late nineteenth and early twentieth centuries. Today, the term *Bushmen* is no longer used, and the preferred name is *San*.

Left: **This young San girl will learn about her future role within her clan by watching her mother and other adult females carry out their daily tasks.**

THE SAN'S HUNTING SKILLS

The hunting skills (*left*) of the San are remarkable because the hunters are able to read the ground as if they were reading a book. San hunters can determine which animals have passed by, as well as their age and sex, by reading signs the animals leave behind. They even notice if a blade of grass has been bent or a spiderweb disturbed. Once an animal has been tracked, the San shoot it with a poisoned arrow.

The San Way of Life

San life centers around bands of several families, usually totaling between twenty-five to sixty people. Individual families within a band are made up of a husband and wife and their dependent children. Most of the band members are related to one another. San bands do not have chiefs, and decisions are made communally within the group.

San religion involves the belief of two supernatural beings. The first is the creator of the world and of living things. The second being represents sickness and death.

The San live in semicircular-shaped huts made of branches and covered with twigs and grass. Their equipment is portable, and they have few possessions. They make their clothes, carrying bags, water containers, and hunting weapons from wood, reeds, and animals.

Women are in charge of food gathering and collect fruits, wild vegetables, and nuts. Men are responsible for hunting animals, such as antelopes, kudus, and gemsboks. For hunting, men use bows and poisoned arrows, as well as snares and spears. The San are famous for their knowledge of poisons. They know which plants contain poison and also use scorpion, snake, spider, and beetle poisons to coat their arrows.

Shaka, Pride of the Warrior Zulus

When Shaka became chief of the Zulu tribe in 1816, the Zulus were a small, insignificant tribe. Under Shaka's leadership, however, the Zulus became a powerful fighting force and established one of Africa's mightiest empires.

Born c. 1787, Shaka was the son of Senzangakona, the Zulu chieftain. At the age of twenty-three, Shaka was called up for military service, and, for six years, he served brilliantly as a warrior. When his father died in 1816, Shaka took over the Zulu clan. At that time, the Zulus were one of the smallest Nguni tribes, numbering less than fifteen hundred. Shaka ruled with brutal force from the start and silenced opposition with instant death.

Shaka's first act as the Zulu chieftain was to reorganize the clan's army into a formidable military machine. He introduced long-bladed assegais, or iron-tipped spears, which revolutionized Nguni fighting tactics. Warriors no longer threw spears at the enemy from a distance; instead they fought at close quarters. The army was also restructured according to age groups and accommodated at separate kraals. Each group was identified by special markings on their shields and various combinations of headdress and ornaments.

Shaka developed battle strategies that were to make his army virtually invincible and build him an empire. Zulu foot warriors, collectively known as the *impi* (IM-pee), covered 50 miles (80 km) a day. Shaka's aim was to defeat all neighboring clans and incorporate those who were not killed into the Zulu clan. In less than a year, Shaka quadrupled the number of his subjects and soldiers, as well as Zulu territories in present-day KwaZulu Natal. Next, Shaka proceeded to conquer clans living south of these territories.

In 1827, Shaka's mother died. Deeply affected by her death, Shaka's military strategies became clouded with poor judgment. As a result, Shaka was murdered by his half brothers in September 1828, but the Zulu empire continued to be strong until its defeat by the Boers at the Battle of Blood River in 1838.

Above: **This drawing shows members of Shaka's impi in full warrior dress, including elaborate feather headdresses.**

MFECANE

Shaka's military exploits led indirectly to the *mfecane* (um-feh-KAH-neh), a period of warfare and forced migrations among southern African peoples. The mfecane caused immense suffering and devastated large areas of South Africa's inland plateau, as clans fled the advancing Zulu armies. Uprooted peoples also fought each other in search of new lands on which to settle. This migration eventually broke the clan structure of the interior and left two million people dead.

Opposite: **This is an artist's impression of Shaka, the great Zulu chieftain, negotiating with the Boers in 1824.**

The South African War

On the Road to War

Although conflicts between the Dutch-descended Boers and the British settlers were long standing, ill feeling grew after the discovery of diamonds and gold in the Boer republics. The Boers resented the influx of mainly British immigrants into the republics and the British government's demand for these British immigrants to have equal political rights. Subsequent negotiations between Paul Kruger, the Boer president of the Transvaal, and the British government failed to solve the problems, and tensions mounted even further. Britain's refusal to withdraw troops from the Transvaal frontiers led the Boer republics of the Transvaal and Orange Free State to declare war on October 12, 1899.

At War

Britain anticipated a quick victory, as its soldiers numbered 500,000, while the Boers had only 87,000. The British soldiers, however, were fighting in unfamiliar territory against an army that had support from the local population.

FAMOUS MEN AND THE SOUTH AFRICAN WAR

Several famous men were involved in the South African War. Mahatma Gandhi raised an ambulance corps of eleven hundred volunteers; he believed Indians living in Natal should help defend the British crown colony. Sir Arthur Conan Doyle, physician and author of *Sherlock Holmes*, worked in a field hospital in Bloemfontein and was knighted for his efforts in 1902. Sir Winston Churchill, working as a journalist for the *Morning Post*, was sent to South Africa to cover the war. He became famous when he took part in rescuing an armored train that had been ambushed by the Boers, although this resulted in his being taken prisoner. Churchill escaped from prison and returned to Britain a military hero.

Left: Three Boer soldiers pose for a photo in 1901. Although many of the Boer soldiers did not have military training, they fought with an intense passion to defend what they believed to be rightfully theirs.

ANGEL OF LOVE

Born in Cornwall, England, in 1860, Emily Hobhouse dedicated her life to helping the less fortunate. When the South African War broke out in 1899, Hobhouse spoke out in opposition. After hearing about the high mortality rates in the British concentration camps, Hobhouse went to South Africa to investigate. She visited some of the camps in the southern part of the country and was appalled at what she saw. She immediately set about finding ways to improve overall living conditions in the camps. Hobhouse also offered help and support to the many imprisoned Boer women, thus earning the nickname "Angel of Love."

Despite initial victories against the British, the Boers were unable to maintain their position. Under the command of Frederick S. Roberts, British troops advanced, and by 1900 they occupied Bloemfontein, Johannesburg, and Pretoria.

Believing the war to be over, Roberts returned to Britain in 1901. The Boers, however, were far from surrendering. Boer leaders, among them future statesmen Louis Botha and Jan Christiaan Smuts, launched extensive and well-planned guerilla warfare against the occupying British forces that lasted another fifteen months. In retaliation, the new British commander in chief, Lord Horatio Herbert Kitchener, adopted severe tactics, known as the scorched earth policy, against the Boer guerillas and the rural population supporting them. Boer and African farms were burned down, and African and Boer women and children were placed in concentration camps.

Exhausted and demoralized, the Boers surrendered in 1902, and the war ended with the Peace of Vereeniging.

The Southern Right Whale

Two species of right whales exist in the world's seas. The northern right whale lives in the Northern Hemisphere, while the southern right whale makes its home in the Southern Hemisphere. Over time, these two types of whales were hunted to the brink of extinction until both species were put under international protection.

The southern right whale is black with white patches on its belly. The whale can grow to 60 feet (18 m) in length and weigh up to 60 tons (54 m tonnes). One characteristic of this species is the growth of callosities, or hard skin, on the front of the head. These growths form patterns that are unique to each whale and help scientists identify individuals. The southern right whale is a baleen whale, which means it has long plates hanging from the top jaw instead of teeth. These baleens work like a sieve when the whale feeds. It eats plankton and small, shrimplike creatures while skimming open-mouthed through the water.

BREATHING METHODS

When the right whale wants to breathe, it surfaces and breathes through two separate blowholes, or nostrils, on top of its head. The spray that comes out of the blowholes forms a 16-foot (4.9-m)-high V shape. The spray consists of warm air, oily secretions from the linings of the whale's airways and lungs, and water vapor produced when the warm breath makes contact with the cooler air. The whale's breathing makes a very loud blowing sound.

Left: Making its home temporarily along the southern coast of South Africa, this southern right whale is leaping into the air and twisting its body before crashing back into the sea with a big, noisy splash. Because the whale's eyes are situated low on its head, the whale must lift its head vertically out of the water to see.

The southern right whale is a migratory whale, which means it spends half the year in one place and the rest of the year in another. It travels long distances between these two places at a speed of about 6 miles (10 km) per hour. In winter, the southern right whale migrates from the waters off Antarctica to the warm waters of the South African shoreline to mate and calf. After being pregnant for about ten months, a female southern right whale produces a single baby. A typical southern right whale gives birth every three years. The mother feeds the baby for about fourteen months, and a young calf can drink up to 159 gallons (600 liters) of milk a day.

Until recently, the largest threat to the survival of the southern right whale has been human predation. It was one of the first whale species to be depleted because it was easy to hunt. Since the implementation of measures designed to protect the species, the southern right whale population has increased from 100 in 1935 to between 1,700 and 2,000 by the 1990s. This number grows by about 7 percent every year.

Although the southern right whale is no longer endangered, the species is still listed as "conservation dependent" by the World Wildlife Fund. It remains to be seen whether the southern right whale population will make a successful comeback.

Above: Hermanus is a popular place for whale watching. Different types of whales, including the southern right whale, can be sighted from the cliffs at the edge of the town. Hermanus is also the location of an annual whale festival.

Three National Parks

Kruger National Park

With an area of 7,722 square miles (20,000 square km), Kruger National Park is one of the ten largest national parks in the world and the biggest game reserve in South Africa. Located in the northeastern part of the country, the park is a savanna region, with a mixture of trees and grassland. Denser subtropical forest, however, can be found along the six permanent rivers that flow through the park.

An enormous variety of wildlife makes its home in the park, including 147 species of mammals, 507 bird species, 114 reptile species, 50 fish species, and 33 amphibian species. Among the most popular attractions are the Big Five, after both black and white rhinoceroses were reintroduced successfully to the park. Other animals include giraffes, zebras, and various kinds of African antelope, such as impalas, wildebeests, and waterbuck.

SOUTH AFRICA'S FIRST NATIONAL PARK

Opened to the public in 1927, Kruger National Park was named after Paul Kruger, president of the Boer republic of the Transvaal. Kruger worked hard to preserve wildlife threatened by overhunting and the expansion of agriculture and mining.

Left: A solitary elephant roams through shrubbery in Addo Elephant National Park. The park not only sustains elephants but also supports a number of antelope, over 170 recorded bird species, and many reptile, amphibian, and insect species.

Opposite: Tourists on safari in Kruger National Park view the park's wildlife from the safety of a vehicle. The more adventurous can explore the park on foot along one of the five wilderness trails. The park has more than six thousand visitors a day.

Tsitsikamma National Park

Made up of a narrow coastal plain flanked by cliffs and beaches, Tsitsikamma National Park is Africa's first marine park. Its name comes from the Hottentot phrase *tse-tsesa gami* (tzhe-tzhe GAH-me), which means "clear water." The park encompasses 50 miles (80 km) of rocky coastline with breathtaking sea- and landscapes, evergreen forests, and deep river gorges. The park also stretches about 3 miles (5 km) out to sea. Visitors may encounter bushbuck, baboons, and otters on the nature trails or follow the snorkeling and scuba trail and be introduced to an underwater world inhabited by fascinating marine creatures.

Addo Elephant National Park

Situated in Eastern Cape, Addo Elephant National Park represents one of South Africa's major conservation success stories. Since the establishment of the park in 1931, the last eleven elephants in the region have grown to over two hundred. The park also offers sanctuary to the last Cape buffalo, as well as the extremely rare black rhinoceros.

THE PLIGHT OF THE EASTERN CAPE ELEPHANTS

In the nineteenth century, great herds of elephants roamed the area north of Port Elizabeth. These huge animals, however, were ruthlessly hunted for their ivory tusks. They were also victims of a deliberate extermination campaign by farmers wishing to protect their land from these roaming animals. Consequently, elephant numbers in the region dwindled rapidly.

Traditional Medicines

During the period of apartheid, modern medicine was not always accessible to black South Africans. Consequently, traditional healers were and still are frequently used and trusted by this portion of the population. Today, it is estimated that over 80 percent of black South Africans visit traditional healers on a regular basis and use the locally available herbal preparations prescribed.

Herbal Remedies

African people have extensive knowledge of trees and shrubs that can be used for different illnesses. Many trees have antibiotic effects, while others can cause numbness and be used for toothaches. Plants also play important roles in traditional medicine. Devil's claw is common in the southern and eastern parts of Africa. The plant is used to ease digestive ailments, reduce fevers, and relieve arthritis and rheumatism, as well as headaches.

Below: **These market vendors in Johannesburg display goods used to prepare traditional herbal remedies. An important ingredient used in many of these remedies is the velvet bushwillow tree. The tree's roots and leaves are used as an antidote for snakebites, and the bark cooked in water soothes stomach disorders.**

Traditional Healers in Modern Society

Approximately 300,000 traditional healers are scattered throughout South Africa. The country's traditional healers include *inyangas* (in-YANG-ahs), who create and prescribe herbal medicines, and *sangomas* (sang-GOH-mahs), who rely on divination as part of their healing. Traditional healers are specialists in botany who, with no formal training, possess incredible knowledge of the chemistry and nutritional and medicinal value of hundreds of herbs. Approximately three quarters of the plant-derived prescription drugs in common use today were discovered by following African remedies that have been handed down from generation to generation.

While remaining enormously popular with the indigenous population, traditional healers are regarded somewhat skeptically by doctors practicing modern medicine. Nevertheless, these traditional healers form the backbone of the primary health care system on which many South Africans rely. Consequently, modern doctors and conservationists are trying to work with traditional healers in such areas as protecting natural resources, as well as addressing specific aspects of health care, including AIDS awareness and education.

Above: These workers in a Johannesburg medicine shop are grinding and bagging tree roots and plants. Many of these plants are gathered and harvested according to strict laws that govern when, where, and how much may be removed at a certain time.

TRAMED

In 1994, a traditional medicines program (TRAMED) was started at the University of Cape Town. The program aims to promote the health, environmental, scientific, and economic benefits that can be obtained from developing, conserving, and using eastern and southern African medicinal plants.

Women in the New South Africa

Women have always been active in shaping South African society, and they played an important role in the struggle against apartheid. Since the end of apartheid, women have concentrated their efforts on fighting for gender equality and women's rights.

The legal standing of South African women improved considerably with the 1993 constitution. Since then, various laws have been passed to protect women from exploitation and give them equal opportunities. The country's South African National Defence Force (SANDF) is also one of the few armed forces in the world that acknowledges the right of South African women to serve in all ranks and positions, including combat roles. At present, women make up 13 percent of the SANDF.

Women are also well-represented in government. At 30 percent, the South African Parliament has the seventh-highest number of women members in all the parliaments in the world. In addition, a woman, Dr. Frene Ginwala, is the current speaker of the National Assembly.

THE REPEAL AND INTRODUCTION OF NEW LAWS

Until December 1993, women's rights in South Africa were limited. Husbands had marital power over their wives and their wives' property, and only fathers had guardianship rights over their children. These inequalities were redressed with the repeal of the General Law Amendment Act and the introduction of the Guardianship Act in 1994. Furthermore, the 1997 Employment Equity Bill disallows discrimination by employers with regard to race, gender, or disability. The Labor Relations Act recognizes women's rights against harassment in the workplace, as well as maternity rights.

Left: As South African women become increasingly independent, a growing number of young women have chosen careers in the South Africa Police Service (SAPS).

Left: **Two women workers help male workers pick tea in a lush, green field in the northeastern part of South Africa.**

Many nongovernmental organizations dealing with women's rights and gender issues are playing an increasingly prominent role in the development of civil society in South Africa. These organizations are actively involved in numerous projects that provide women with opportunities to learn useful skills ranging from computer literacy to learning how to build and finance a house. The latter is of vital importance to the many women who live in makeshift huts of cardboard and corrugated iron in or around South Africa's cities and towns.

Many South African women, however, still have a long way to go before they achieve some form of liberation from their traditional roles in society. Women who are subject to customary law still do not have full legal rights and are not treated as adults. Customary law is based on indigenous law and practice. African women married under this system have no property rights and no access to the regular courts.

Furthermore, millions of women and children continue to live in poverty in shantytowns that have neither running water nor electricity. Consequently, these women have to hike long distances to fetch water and firewood every day. Despite the increase in job opportunities for South African women, most women living in these areas are unemployed or earn very low wages doing menial jobs.

Below: **Many rural South African women are responsible for tending crops. This woman is watering crops in the country's northeastern region.**

Zulu Beadwork

Zulu beadwork is unique because it serves as an intricate means of personal and social communication. The choice and combination of colors and geometric designs have special meanings and are used to express feelings, circumstances, and behavior, as well as relationships between men and women.

An exclusively feminine art, beadwork and the meaning of the symbols and colors used are passed on to young girls by their older sisters or mothers. Beaded items are usually worn as a head- or neckband by girls and women who wish to communicate certain information. With the help of female relatives to explain the codes, a man can see whether a woman is single, engaged, or married or has children or unmarried sisters. The patterns and colors also reveal from which region a woman comes and her social standing in the community.

The basic geometric shape used for this type of beadwork is the triangle. The three corners of the triangle represent the family:

Opposite: **Colorful beaded head- and neckbands are sold widely throughout South Africa.**

Below: **This Zulu woman is busy threading beads to make a colorful neckband. For Zulu women, beadwork is a symbol of their social status as well as an opportunity to express their creativity.**

father, mother, and child. If the point of the triangle faces down, it stands for an unmarried man or boy. If, however, the point of the triangle faces up, it represents an unmarried woman or girl. Two triangles joined at the point, thus forming an hourglass shape, symbolize a married man, while two triangles joined at the base to form a diamond shape represent a married woman.

Seven colors are used in Zulu beadwork — black, blue, yellow, green, pink, red, and white. Except for white, each color has two meanings, one positive and one negative. White has only one meaning — purity and love. When a color is used alongside white, the color takes on a positive meaning. For example, a blue band and a white band symbolize fidelity or fertility. Blue, white, and black bands represent marriage.

Transitions in life are celebrated by wearing specially crafted bead wear. When a woman is engaged, she wears a 16-foot (5-m)-long white beaded necklace adorned with blue and white tassels. A married woman wears a headdress with the geometric sign that denotes her status. A leather-backed beaded belt decorated with geometric designs is worn by new mothers, while a woman who has children wears a necklace that has large beads representing fertility.

LOVE LETTERS

A young Zulu woman will give a young man she is fond of a beaded necklace with small patterned panels. These necklaces are commonly known as *incwadi kuthanda* (INTZ-vah-dee koo-TON-dah), or love letters. The color code and design of each necklace contains a special message for the recipient. If the young man returns the affection of the young woman, he will make this known in public by wearing the necklace at a communal celebration. Once a couple is courting, the Zulu woman continues to use beaded love letters to communicate with her suitor.

RELATIONS WITH NORTH AMERICA

In recent history, relations between South Africa and North America were severely affected by South Africa's policy of apartheid. North American opposition to South Africa's system of apartheid grew increasingly during the 1970s and 1980s. This opposition culminated in both the United States and Canada supporting sanctions imposed by the international community as a protest against South Africa's racial policies.

Since South Africa's first historic, democratic elections in April 1994 and the lifting of international sanctions, North America has reestablished full relations with South Africa.

Below: U.S. president Bill Clinton (*left*) applauds newly elected South African president Nelson Mandela (*right*) during a speech made by Mandela in Washington, D.C., in May 1994. During his visit to the United States, Mandela invited the United States to recommence trading with his country.

The three countries enjoy good trade relations, and South Africa has benefitted immensely from North American investment in South African businesses.

South Africa has also received funding from the United States and Canada in the area of humanitarian aid. Today, North American aid agencies work with organizations in South Africa to improve the South African people's quality of life. South African culture has also had a lasting impact on North American culture, especially in the arts.

Opposite: This woman stands in front of an advertisement for Coca-Cola after buying two big bags of snacks at a market in Soweto.

Historical Ties

Relations between South Africa and the United States began officially in 1799 when an American consulate was opened in Cape Town. Trade between the two countries developed significantly after 1867, when diamonds were discovered in the Boer republic of Orange Free State.

During the South African War, 7,368 Canadian troops were sent to South Africa to help British forces in their fight against the Boers. It was the first time Canadian, Australian, and New Zealand units fought overseas in an imperial war. Along with the United States, Canada and South Africa, both of which were members of the then British Empire, were among the founding members of the League of Nations in 1919. This international organization was established to peacefully settle disputes between nations. South African forces also fought on the Allied side during World Wars I and II.

The establishment of the Commonwealth and the U.N. in 1931 and 1945, respectively, drew the Canadian and South African governments closer together. This closeness, however, did not last because of differences on issues and policies. By 1948, Canada made it clear that it did not support South Africa's racial polices, and the country played a key role in forcing South Africa to withdraw from the Commonwealth in 1961.

CANADIAN PRESSURE MOUNTS

In the late 1970s, Canada increased pressure on South Africa to end apartheid. The Canadian government withdrew its trade commissioners from Johannesburg and Cape Town, closed the Canadian consulate general in Johannesburg, and stopped Export Development Corporation aid to South African-Canadian trading companies. In addition, Canada participated in the Commonwealth sports boycott that stopped Commonwealth teams from competing in South Africa or against South African teams.

Left: A World War I veteran looks at the Remembrance Day poster unveiled on October 14, 1999, in Ottawa. The poster marks a "Century of Valor" and features photographs of Canadian men and women who served in the South African War, World Wars I and II, and international peacekeeping missions.

76

By the 1970s, North American-South African relations were severely affected, as the United States and Canada joined the international community in condemning apartheid. In 1974, South Africa was excluded from the U.N. General Assembly.

International efforts to end apartheid intensified in the 1980s, and both the Canadian and U.S. governments declared sanctions against South Africa in 1985 and 1986, respectively. North American investment in the country dropped, and many North American companies pulled out of South Africa. The United States and Canada also began to support educational upgrading and other programs designed to promote a more equal South Africa. Aid for all of these programs was channeled through nongovernmental organizations and bypassed the South African government.

With the end of apartheid and the release of Nelson Mandela in 1990, both the United States and Canada played major roles in the preparation for South Africa's first nonracial elections in April 1994. The United States was the largest donor in assisting with the election process. Hundreds of North Americans participated as U.N. and international observers of the 1994 elections. Since then, sanctions, including those imposed by the United States and Canada, have been lifted. South Africa rejoined the Commonwealth on June 1, 1994, and its credentials to the U.N. General Assembly were accepted on June 23, 1994.

FROM U.S. SANCTIONS TO ELECTION AID

In response to the growing opposition to apartheid among the American population, the U.S. Congress passed the Comprehensive Anti-Apartheid Act in 1986. This act authorized federal sanctions on imports and exports.

Measures in the Anti-Apartheid Act were lifted with the end of apartheid, and President Bill Clinton signed into law the South African Democratic Transition Support Act. Provisions in the act allowed the United States to support the strengthening of the South African electoral machinery. Consequently, over a two-year period prior to South Africa's first nonracial elections, the United States provided $35 million to nongovernmental organizations to support voter education, political party training, and training for election monitors in South Africa. Efforts were focused especially in the rural areas and among disadvantaged groups, such as women, where the needs were greatest.

Current Relations

Since the lifting of international sanctions against South Africa, trade and investment relations have improved between South Africa and North America. Today, the United States is one of South Africa's key trading partners, and South African exports to the United States rose from U.S. $645 million in 1993 to U.S. $1.8 billion in 1998. Trade and investment between South Africa and the United States was further strengthened with the founding of the U.S.-South Africa Binational Commission in 1995. The commission is designed to promote cooperation between the two countries in areas such as trade and investment, agriculture, education, conservation and the environment, and defense.

Canada is another important trading partner. Since 1994, bilateral trade has increased from U.S. $94 million in 1993 to U.S. $373 million in 1998. In September 1998, the Trade and Investment Co-operation Arrangement (TICA) was signed between the two countries. TICA established the Consultative Group on Trade and Investment Co-operation to promote trade and investment between the two countries and to deal with issues of concern and the fostering of business links in key sectors. Canada also hopes to strengthen its existing trade

SACCO

The South African Canada Council (SACCO) was formed to promote, encourage, and facilitate commercial, social, and cultural relations between South Africa and Canada and to foster goodwill between the two nations.

and investment ties with South Africa, especially in areas such as agriculture, mining, and telecommunications. Today, over seventy-five Canadian firms have set up offices in South Africa or participated in joint ventures with South African partners. Canada is also one of the largest providers of development assistance to South Africa and has rendered valuable assistance in the fields of education and training, law, and the environment.

State Visits

In March 1998, President Bill Clinton became the first U.S. president to visit South Africa while in office. In September 1998, then South African president Nelson Mandela paid an official visit to the United States, which included an address to leading business executives and a visit to Harvard University. During his visit, President Mandela was awarded the Congressional Gold Medal, the United States's highest civilian honor. President Mandela then went on to pay a state visit to Canada, where he became the first foreign leader to be given the title of Honorary Companion of Order of Canada, the country's highest award.

Below: Canadian prime minister Jean Chretien (*left*) applauds as South Africa's president Nelson Mandela (*center*) is congratulated by Governor General Romeo LeBlanc (*right*) after he received an Honorary Companion of Order of Canada at a ceremony in Ottawa on September 24, 1998. Mandela made a state visit to Canada as part of a farewell tour to North America before retiring as president in 1999.

Humanitarian Ties

South Africa, the United States, and Canada are members of various organizations, such as the U.N., the United Nations Educational, Scientific, and Cultural Organization (UNESCO), and the World Health Organization (WHO), that strive to help improve the lives of people around the world.

North American and South African troops work together on numerous peacekeeping missions in troubled areas of the world. At present, U.S., Canadian, and South African troops are among peacekeeping troops monitoring the cease-fire between the warring countries of Ethiopia and Eritrea.

North American Development Agencies

Major North American development agencies present in South Africa are the U.S. Agency for International Development (USAID) and the Canadian International Development Agency

Left: **South Africa's ambassador to the United States, Sheila Violet Makate Sisulu (*foreground*), speaks at a U.N. press conference held on June 6, 2001, in New York City, as Dr. Henry McKinnell (*behind*), president of the pharmaceutical company Pfizer Inc., listens. Pfizer announced that it would provide diflucan antifungal medicine at no charge to HIV/AIDS patients in fifty developing countries, as identified by the U.N., where HIV/AIDS is most widespread.**

(CIDA). Both agencies bring together many people from the United States and Canada to work toward improving health care and living conditions in developing countries.

The Canadian and U.S. governments support South Africa's Reconstruction and Development Programme (RDP) through CIDA and USAID, respectively. Both countries make considerable contributions to the program, and the areas of focus include democracy and exercise of authority, reform in the education and health systems, and economic development.

Peace Corps South Africa

Established in 1961, the Peace Corps is a U.S. governmental agency of volunteers who work in countries all over the world to improve education, health, agriculture, trade, and business. In 1995, U.S. president Bill Clinton and South African president Nelson Mandela signed an agreement that made South Africa the 131st country the Peace Corps has entered. First arriving in South Africa in 1997, Peace Corps volunteers work in Northern and Mpumalanga provinces. One of the main aims of Peace Corps South Africa's volunteers is to help train people of all ages, as well as improve the teaching of English, science, and mathematics. The volunteers are also involved in other community-generated projects, such as HIV/AIDS awareness.

Left: **Three young Canadians watch as South African Donald Montoedi (*seated*) signs the Montréal city hall guest book at the launch of a program supported by the Canadian government to promote racial equality in Canada.**

South Africans in North America

During the years of apartheid, many South Africans fled their homeland, choosing either the United States or Canada as their destination. Some moved in the hope of finding a better life, others were forced to live in exile because of their political beliefs. Today, the United States and Canada are two of the five countries that collectively account for three quarters of South African emigration.

South Africans have settled all over the United States, including New York, Boston, Los Angeles, and Minnesota. In Canada, 56 percent of South African immigrants live in Ontario, primarily in Toronto. Other South African communities are in Vancouver and Montréal.

South Africans living in the United States and Canada have set up numerous clubs and organizations, such as the Canadian Council of South Africans (CANCOSA), that encourage the growth of a vibrant and united South African community and strengthen links between the old and new homelands. South Africans also keep in touch with news related to their homeland by reading South African newspapers, magazines, and newsletters. One such newsletter is *Juluka.* Published monthly in the United States, the newsletter aims to help South Africans adapt to their new way of life.

THE HOUSE HUSBAND

The play *The House Husband*, written by Durban actor Aldo Brincat, has caught the imagination of the South African public with its fresh perspective on the issue of South African emigration. The play takes a tragicomic look at a South African who has emigrated to Canada and is struggling with his wife's failure to adapt to their new life. Brincat's inspiration for the play was the large number of friends and colleagues who have emigrated and the impact this has had on his and their relationships.

North Americans in South Africa

The number of North Americans living in South Africa is very small. Most North Americans who go to South Africa are there on vacation, for business purposes, or as members of voluntary aid agencies.

South Africa is now rated by the World Tourism Organization as one of the top tourist destinations in the world, and Cape Town is rated one of the world's top ten tourist destination cities. The number of North American tourists visiting the country has been increasing steadily since 1994. Popular destinations include Cape Town, world-famous national parks, and the country's beautiful beaches. North American tourists are also venturing into the former homelands, where they have the chance to stay in bed and breakfasts run by residents. There, they experience firsthand the everyday hardships endured by many black South Africans.

Canada and the United States both have embassies in Pretoria. Furthermore, the Canadian Alliance for Business in Southern Africa has been operating since 1996 and establishes business links and technology transfers between Canadian and South African companies.

Below: **Today, South Africa's varied landscapes and diverse cultures are attracting North American tourists in increasing numbers. While in the country, many tourists try a number of exciting water sports, such as white-water rafting.**

South Africa in Hollywood

Opposition to apartheid also made its way into Hollywood. Throughout the 1980s and early 1990s, a number of Hollywood movies, some of which became box-office hits, touched on this sensitive political issue.

Cry Freedom (1987), starring Kevin Kline and Denzel Washington, was one of the first movies to bring the horrors of apartheid to mass cinema audiences. The movie dealt with the friendship formed between a white South African journalist and the black activist Stephen Biko. The theme of apartheid also was interwoven into the storyline for *Lethal Weapon II* (1989), which starred Mel Gibson and Danny Glover. Another touching movie that was set during the apartheid years but released in 1992 was the musical *Sarafina!* Directed by South African Darrell James Roodt and starring Whoopi Goldberg and South African singer Zensi Miriam Makeba, the movie tells the story of a young girl caught up in the struggle for freedom in South Africa just before the release of Nelson Mandela and the end of apartheid. Roodt then went on to direct a remake of the moving film *Cry the Beloved Country*, starring Richard Harris and James Earl Jones, in 1995.

Above: This scene is from the movie *Cry the Beloved Country* featuring Richard Harris (*left*) and James Earl Jones (*right*). South African music is featured on the movie's soundtrack.

CHARLIZE THERON

One successful South African actress is Charlize Theron. Born in 1975, Theron moved to Hollywood to pursue her career in acting. She has starred alongside Al Pacino and Keanu Reeves in *Devil's Advocate* (1997), Johnny Depp in *The Astronaut's Wife*, and Sir Michael Caine in the critically acclaimed *The Cider House Rules* (1999).

Music

South African music first made an impact on North American audiences in the 1960s with hits by Hugh Masekela and Miriam Makeba. South African music again hit the world music scene and became hugely popular with North American audiences with the release of singer and songwriter Paul Simon's *Graceland* album in 1986. Big names in South African music collaborated with Simon on the project, including bassist Bakithi Kumalo and internationally known Masekela and Makeba. *Graceland* also created international interest in groups such as Ladysmith Black Mambazo. Since 1986, the band has gone on to enjoy success in the United States and has performed with many American artists.

South African music has also reached the big screen. The music for the Walt Disney movie *The Lion King* (1994) was inspired by Zulu music, and the song "One by One" featured in the movie is a prime example of iscathamiya. *The Lion King Part II: Simba's Pride* (1998) also featured music by Ladysmith Black Mambazo.

Below: Paul Simon (*fifth from left*) and Ladysmith Black Mambazo recorded the song "Put down the Duckie" for the popular children's television show *Sesame Street* in 1987.

SOUTH AFRICA

Tropic of Capricorn

B O T S W A N A

N A M I B I A

K A L A H A R I

K a l a h a r i

D e s e r t

NORTH-WEST

Witwatersrand

GAUTENG

■ **PRET**

● **Soweto**　● **Johann**

● **Vereenigin**

● **Sharpeville**

MIDDLE-VELD

H I G H V E L D

Harts

Vaal

N

Orange

FREE STATE

● **Kimberley**

Mount Njesuthi
(11,182 feet / 3,408 m)

● **Bloemfontein**

LESOTHO

NORTHERN CAPE

G R E A T

Fish

E S C A R P M E N T

Orange

Drake

EASTERN CAPE

Wild

ATLANTIC OCEAN

Robben Island

Cape Floristic Region

WESTERN CAPE

● **East Londor**

● **Grahamstown**

Addo Elephant National Park

● **Port Elizabeth**

● **Cape Town**

Hout Bay ●

Cape Point

Hermanus

Cape of Good Hope

Tsitsikamma National Park

● **Mossel Bay**

Cape L'Agulhas

I N D I A N

O C E A N

Above: The Drakensberg Mountains offer breathtaking views of South Africa.

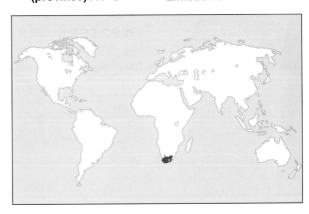

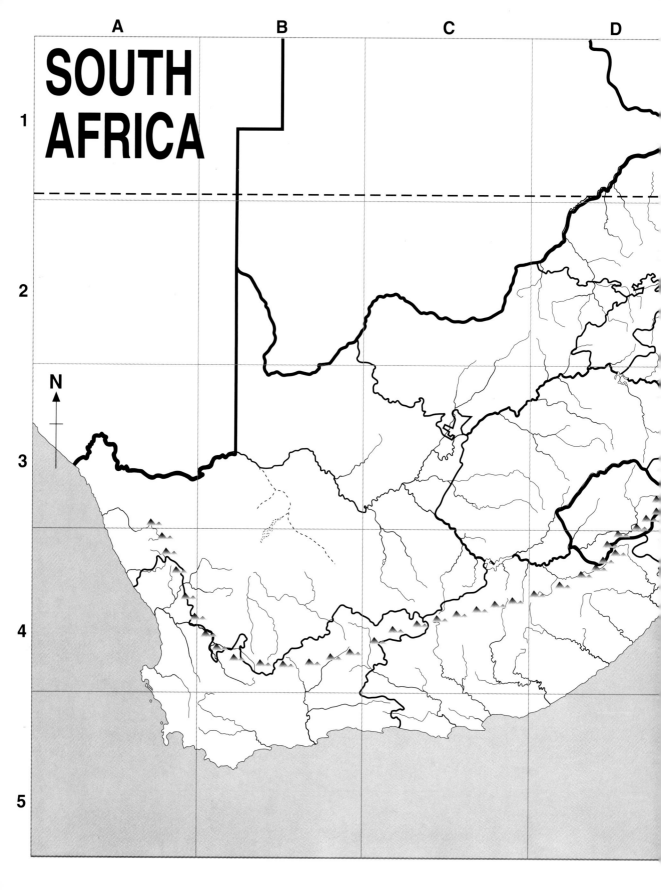

SOUTH AFRICA

A   B   C   D

1

2

N

3

4

5

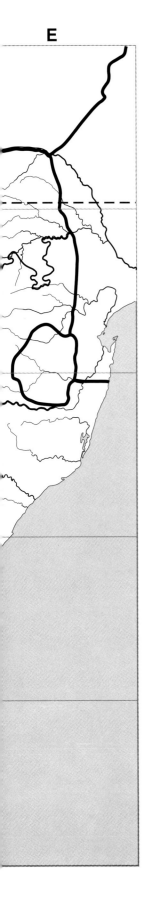

E

How Is Your Geography?

Learning to identify the main geographical areas and points of a country can be challenging. Although it may seem difficult at first to memorize the locations and spellings of major cities or the names of mountain ranges, rivers, deserts, lakes, and other prominent physical features, the end result of this effort can be very rewarding. Places you previously did not know existed will suddenly come to life when referred to in world news, whether in newspapers, television reports, or other books and reference sources. This knowledge will make you feel a bit closer to the rest of the world, with its fascinating variety of cultures and physical geography.

Used in a classroom setting, the instructor can make duplicates of this map using a copy machine. (PLEASE DO NOT WRITE IN THIS BOOK!) Students can then fill in any requested information on their individual map copies. Used one-on-one, the student can also make copies of the map on a copy machine and use them as a study tool. The student can practice identifying place names and geographical features on his or her own.

Below: **The buildings surrounding Cape Town's harbor are a mixture of traditional and modern architectural styles.**

South Africa at a Glance

Official Name   Republic of South Africa

Capital Cities   Pretoria (executive capital)

     Bloemfontein (judicial capital)

     Cape Town (legislative capital)

Official Languages   Afrikaans, English, Ndebele, Pedi, Sotho, Swazi, Tsonga, Tswana, Venda, Xhosa, Zulu

Population   43,421,021 (2000 estimate)

Land Area   471,008 square miles (1,219,912 square km)

Provinces   Eastern Cape, Free State, Gauteng, KwaZulu Natal, Mpumalanga, North-West, Northern, Northern Cape, Western Cape

Highest Point   Mount Njesuthi 11,182 feet (3,408 m)

Border Countries   Botswana, Lesotho, Mozambique, Namibia, Swaziland, Zimbabwe

Major Rivers   Limpopo, Orange, Vaal

Major Cities   Bloemfontein, Cape Town, Durban, Johannesburg, Kimberley, Port Elizabeth, Pretoria

Major Religions   Christianity, animism, Islam, Hinduism, Judaism, traditional beliefs

National Holidays   Human Rights' Day (March 21), Freedom Day (April 27), Youth Day (June 16), National Women's Day (August 9), Day of Reconciliation (December 16)

Major Exports   Diamonds, gold, machinery and equipment, other metals and minerals

Major Imports   Chemicals, foodstuffs and equipment, machinery, petroleum products, scientific instruments

Currency   Rand (8.06 ZAR = U.S. $1 in 2001)

Opposite: **This young South African stands near the top of a hill that gently slopes down to the coast along KwaZulu Natal.**

Glossary

Afrikaans Vocabulary

apartheid (ah-PAHRT-hate): separateness; a political system in South Africa that separated people of different races.

biltong (bill-TONG): dried meat.

bobotie (ber-BOW-ah-tee): a baked dish made with minced beef or lamb, onions, spices, and lemon, usually served with yellow rice.

boerewors (BOO-er-vors): farmer's sausage; a spicy sausage made of beef, mutton, or venison.

Boers (BOO-ers): farmers; early Dutch, French, and German settlers.

braaivleis (BREYE-flace): grilling meat; an outdoor gathering at which meat is grilled over an open fire; a barbecue.

bredies (BREAR-dees): stews.

breyani (bray-AH-nee): spicy rice with lentils, vegetables, and fish, chicken, or mutton.

koeksuster (COOK-sis-ter): a twisted doughnut fried in oil and covered in syrup.

kraals (KRAHLS): Zulu beehive huts made of straw.

melktert (MELK-tairt): a cinnamon-flavored custard tart.

pap (PUP): cornmeal porridge.

sosaties (soh-SAH-tees): marinated kabobs.

technikons (teck-NEE-cons): technical or vocational institutions.

veld (FELT): grassy plains.

waterblommetjie bredi (VAH-ter-bloh-mer-key BREAR-dee): waterlily and lamb stew.

Hottentot Vocabulary

tse-tsesa gami (tzhe-tzhe GAH-me): clear water.

Zulu Vocabulary

impi (IM-pee): Zulu warriors.

incwadi kuthanda (INTZ-vah-dee koo-TON-dah): love letters.

inyangas (in-YANG-ahs): traditional South African healers who create and prescribe herbal medicines.

iscathamiya (is-COT-ah-me-yah): traditional Zulu call-and-response choral music sung without instrumental accompaniment.

kwaito (KWEH-toh): a type of African music that involves remixing international music by slowing the speed and adding local instruments and melodies.

kwela (KWEH-lah): street music played on homemade guitars and pennywhistles.

mbaqanga (um-bah-TZAN-gah): urban African music.

mfecane (um-feh-KAH-neh): crushing; a period of warfare and forced migrations among southern African peoples.

sangomas (sang-GOH-mahs): traditional South African healers who rely on divination as part of their healing.

shebeen (shah-BEEN): public house.

toyi-toyi (TOY-TOY): a militant marching dance.

umngqusho (um-tzuh-GOO-show): a dish made from corn kernels, potatoes, sugar beans, butter, onions, chili, and lemons.

English Vocabulary

amnesty: an official pardon for offenses against a government.

bicameral: having two branches, houses, or chambers as a legislative body.

biodiversity: the diversity of plant and animal species in an environment.

botany: the branch of biology that deals with plant life.

boycott: to join together to stop or prevent dealings with a country, group, or person, as a means of protest.

circumcision: the act of removing the fold of skin covering the genital organs of males or females, especially as a ceremonial or religious rite.

convergence: the process in which ideas, groups, or communities stop being different and become more alike.

depleted: decreased seriously or exhausted the abundance or supply of.

embargo: an order prohibiting commerce with another country.

gables: portions of the front or side of a building, usually triangular in shape, enclosed by roofs that slope downward from a central ridge.

game: wild animals or birds traditionally hunted for food or sporting purposes.

Gothic: a style of architecture characterized by tall pillars; high, curved ceilings; and pointed arches.

homelands: racially and ethnically based regions created by South Africa's apartheid government as nominally independent tribal states.

incarceration: imprisonment.

indigenous: originating in or characteristic of a particular region or country.

infrastructure: bridges, roads, and other basic facilities serving a country.

initiation: the ceremonies or rites of acceptance into a certain group.

innate: inborn.

navigable: describing a body of water deep and large enough to allow ships to pass through it.

neoclassical: a style of architecture that is influenced by Roman and Greek architecture.

nuclear family: a social unit consisting of a father, a mother, and their children.

oppressive: unjustly harsh.

predation: the act of hunting and killing animals for food.

reconciliation: the act of bringing into agreement or harmony.

resurged: reappeared or rose again as from virtual extinction.

sabotage: the destruction of property or obstruction of public services, so as to undermine a government.

sanctions: measures taken by a country to restrict trade and official contact with a nation that has broken international law.

savanna: a plain characterized by coarse grasses and scattered tree growth, especially on the margins of the tropics.

segregation: the separation of different ethnic groups according to skin color.

stakes: areas that are claimed for work or investment, in hopes of gain.

township: a residential settlement for black South Africans, located outside a city or town.

treason: the offense of acting to overthrow a government.

More Books to Read

Mandela: From the Life of the South African Statesman. Floyd Cooper (Philomel Books)

No More Strangers Now: Young Voices from a New South Africa. Tim McKee (DK Publishing)

No Turning Back: A Novel of South Africa. Beverley Naidoo (HarperCollins)

South Africa. Enchantment of the World series. Ettagale Blauer and Jason Lauré (Children's Press)

South Africa. Festivals of the World series. Jay Heale (Gareth Stevens)

South Africa. Major World Nations series. Claudia Canesso and Jeff Beneke (Chelsea House)

South Africa: 1800 to the Present: Imperialism, Nationalism, and Apartheid. Exploration of Africa: The Emerging Nations series. Bruce and Becky Durost Fish (Chelsea House)

South Africa: A Tapestry of Peoples and Traditions. Exploring Cultures of the World series. Jacqueline Drobis Meisel (Benchmark Books)

Videos

The First Free Elections. (SVE and Churchill Media)

Going Places: South Africa. (MPI Home Video)

South Africa: Free at Last. (A & E Home Video)

South African Safari. (Tapeworm)

Web Sites

www.anc.org.za/people/mandela.html

www.krugersafari.com

www.learner.org/exhibits/southafrica/

www.southafrica-newyork.net/consulate/aboutSA.htm

Due to the dynamic nature of the Internet, some web sites stay current longer than others. To find additional web sites, use a reliable search engine with one or more of the following keywords to help you locate information about South Africa. Keywords: *apartheid, Boers, Cape of Good Hope, Johannesburg, Nelson Mandela, Desmond Tutu, Zulus.*

Index